COLLABORATIVE FUTURES IN QUALITATIVE INQUIRY

Collaborative Futures in Qualitative Inquiry critically reflects on and explores the role of qualitative research amidst the global COVID-19 pandemic. Against this unprecedented backdrop, it asks what research means during a global pandemic and what it means to be an academic.

Leading international scholars from the United States, Canada, Chile, New Zealand, Norway, and the United Kingdom wrestle with the changing dynamics of research in pandemic times. Collectively and collaboratively, contributors call for a critical, performative, social justice inquiry directed at the multiple crises of our historical present—a rethinking of where we have been, and, critically, where we are going. More specifically, contributors focus on such topics as: the emotional geographies of academic writing; assaults on science and truth; pedagogies of the imagination; indigenization and reconciliation; the search for our common humanity; and the relevance of qualitative inquiry in an era of big data and digital transformation.

Collaborative Futures in Qualitative Inquiry is a must-read for faculty and students alike who are interested in imagining new ways to collaborate, to engage in research and activism, and represent and intervene into social life in pandemic times.

Norman K. Denzin is Distinguished Emeritus Professor of Communications, Sociology, and the Humanities at the University of Illinois, Urbana–Champaign. He is the Founder of the International Congress of Qualitative Inquiry.

Michael D. Giardina is Professor of Physical Culture and Qualitative Inquiry in the Department of Sport Management at Florida State University. He is the Director of the International Congress of Qualitative Inquiry.

COLLABORATIVE FUTURES IN QUALITATIVE INQUIRY

Research in a Pandemic

*Edited by Norman K. Denzin
and Michael D. Giardina*

Routledge
Taylor & Francis Group

NEW YORK AND LONDON

First published 2021
by Routledge
605 Third Avenue, New York, NY 10158

and by Routledge
2 Park Square, Milton Park, Abingdon, Oxon, OX14 4RN

Routledge is an imprint of the Taylor & Francis Group, an informa business

Library of Congress Cataloging-in-Publication Data
Names: Denzin, Norman K., editor. | Giardina, Michael D., 1976- editor.
Title: Collaborative futures in qualitative inquiry: research in a pandemic/
   edited by Norman K. Denzin and Michael D. Giardina.
Description: New York, NY: Routledge, 2021. | Includes bibliographical
   references and index. |
Identifiers: LCCN 2020053599 (print) | LCCN 2020053600 (ebook) |
   ISBN 9780367723798 (hbk) | ISBN 9780367723835 (pbk) |
   ISBN 9781003154587 (ebk)
Subjects: LCSH: Social sciences–Research. | Qualitative
   research–Methodology.
Classification: LCC H62 .C56565 2021 (print) | LCC H62 (ebook) |
   DDC 300.72/1–dc23
LC record available at https://lccn.loc.gov/2020053599
LC ebook record available at https://lccn.loc.gov/2020053600

ISBN: 978-0-367-72379-8 (hbk)
ISBN: 978-0-367-72383-5 (pbk)
ISBN: 978-1-003-15458-7 (ebk)

Typeset in Bembo
by KnowledgeWorks Global Ltd.

Printed in the United Kingdom
by Henry Ling Limited

CONTENTS

ACKNOWLEDGMENTS

We thank editor-extraordinaire Hannah Shakespeare and Matt Bickerton at Routledge for their support of this volume and the larger ICQI project. Thanks also to Manisha Singh during the copyediting phase. Many of the chapters in this book were scheduled to be presented as plenary or keynote addresses at the sixteenth International Congress of Qualitative Inquiry, which was to be held at the University of Illinois, Urbana-Champaign, in May 2020, but was cancelled due to COVID-19. We thank the Institute of Communications Research, the College of Media, and the International Institute for Qualitative Inquiry for continued support of the Congress.

For information on future Congresses, please visit http://www.icqi.org.

Norman K. Denzin
Michael D. Giardina
November 2020

INTRODUCTION

Norman K. Denzin and Michael D. Giardina

Proem

2020 has been a long decade.
We don't mean that to be flip; it has felt like an eternity.
It has been exhausting.
> Depressing.
>> Stressful.
>>> Ridden with anxiety,
>>>> fear,
>>>>> and hopelessness.
>>>>>> And altogether rather horrible.

In December 2019, impeachment proceedings against U.S. President Donald Trump began; the following month (January 2020), the novel coronavirus SARS-CoV-2 (which causes COVID-19) emerged in the city of Wuhan, China.[1] These twinned vectors in history—a president not interested in the common good (and perhaps even siding with foreign governments in subverting democracy) and buoyed by a particularly insidious brand of nationalist populism, and a highly infectious virus spreading like wildfire across the globe, the likes of which haven't seen since the Spanish Flu epidemic of 1918-1920—have hung over our collective heads as the long, slow march toward 2021 comes to a close.

As the stark, heartbreaking images and stories out of China, and later Italy—the two countries to realize the earliest outbreaks—came to dominate the airwaves and social media, it seemed inevitable that such an easily transmissible virus would make its way around the world. In the United States, it began with Seattle, Washington, and its surrounding suburbs on the West Coast and New York City on the East Coast becoming flashpoints for a looming national calamity. As the spread from these two hot spots gathered steam in the early Spring, federal responses were mixed, inefficient, and rudderless at best, leaving state governments to in many ways and various degrees of success establish their own mitigation guidelines (or lack thereof), impose "lockdowns" and stay-at-home orders (or not), and try to "flatten the growth curve" to buy more time for hospitals and healthcare professionals to ramp up in anticipation for an influx of new cases and hospitalizations. Fear, confusion, and economic upheaval quickly followed: U.S. unemployment rose from a 50-year low of ~3.5% to 14.7% almost overnight (in one four-week period, 22 million Americans filed for unemployment benefits; see Long, 2020), and "real" GDP growth fell by a shocking 31.4% during the second quarter of 2020 (see Patton, 2020).

In March, the COVID-19 crisis reached educational systems (both K-12 and university) throughout the United States[2] and around the world; in what felt like an instant, face-to-face classes became online offerings as schools closed campuses; faculty and committee meetings became one Zoom appointment after another; university administrators seemingly had to write, rewrite, and invent new guidelines and procedures every week to respond to the changing public health landscape; and local school boards wrestled with how to keep children—especially those without ready access to technology or caregivers in families with working parents—progressing forward in coursework and social development. Work-from-home became the new national mantra—one that clearly privileged those in many white-collar industries, whereas service workers and those in mission-critical work (hospitals, grocery stores, public utilities, etc.) were left having to juggle a fickle and feckless free market that has far too often undervalued and underpaid such employees. While some countries implemented a well-managed lockdown and paid workers as much as 80% of salary to "stay home", in the United States thus far the Republican-controlled Senate has provided only a one-time, $1,200 relief benefit in the last 10 months (as part of the CARES Act).

From the start of the pandemic, accurate and accessible testing for SARS-CoV-2 was poorly managed or left to happenstance, with President Trump actively working to minimize testing efforts because, as he stated in his customary incoherence, "When you test, you create more cases" (as if a virus waits for a positive test result in order to wreak havoc on a person). Wearing cloth face coverings—arguably the most important practical defense against contracting SARS-CoV-2 (see Greenhalgh, 2020; Greenhalgh and colleagues, 2020)—became a political hot button issue throughout the United States (though less so in most other parts of the world), splitting, not unsurprisingly, along political affiliation lines, with Democrats largely supporting and encouraging face coverings in public places, and Republicans claiming they were either ineffective or violated their civil liberties (or both)—claims the President himself put forward on a nearly daily basis. With clinical vaccine trials underway throughout the world, but projected to take 18–24 months at best, the President repeatedly argued that the malaria drug Hydroxychloroquine was a magic bullet, though no empirical scientific evidence supported its use. (By the same token, the President suggested during a press conference that *injecting bleach into the human body* would also cleanse it from the disease, which may rank as one of the most asinine things an American president has ever uttered in public.)[3] This was part and parcel with Trump (and Trump administration) attacks on science that have pervaded throughout the last four years—whether related to global warming, gun violence, mental health, or economics.

As the hot summer wore on, the country erupted in protest of all kinds—the public murder of George Floyd (an African American man) by Minneapolis, Minnesota police offers and the murder of Breonna Taylor (an African American woman "accidentally" killed in her own home by police in Texas) serving as flashpoints for renewed calls for justice in the wake of police brutality; the global spread of the Black Lives Matter movement accelerated, bringing the issue into worldwide discussion. Images of increasingly militarized police responses, especially in Washington, D.C., and Portland, Oregon, became front page news, energizing large swaths of the American public to take action—to take to the streets—in numbers heretofore unseen for decades. Alongside this battle for the soul of the country—for a recentering of social justice at the heart of everyday public relations—SARS-CoV-2 advanced unimpeded. Despite the magical thinking (some might say, ignorance or incompetence) of the Trump administration, which made increasingly bizarre claims that it would simply "go away" as it downplayed the seriousness of it all, the coronavirus pandemic ravaged the nation, and, especially communities of color. According to David R. Holtgrave and colleagues (2020), heightened COVID-19 mortality among Black and Hispanic communities has been well established epidemiologically, realizing a 3.48-fold disparity for Hispanic (relative to White) communities, and a 5.38-fold disparity for non-Hispanic Black (relative to White) communities, based primarily on the "infection experience and the need for hospitalization, given infection" (p. 9). Simply stated, racial, ethnic, and socioeconomic disparities both revealed and amplified the gross health(care) inequality in the United States at a time in which the Trump administration was actively working to repeal the Affordable Care Act and protections for preexisting conditions.

To wit, and almost a year into this "new normal", the United States careened toward a Presidential election (more on that in a moment) with daily COVID-19 cases surpassing the 100,000 mark; hospitals in many states were stretched to the brink once again; and parts of the global economy remained in "shock" and suggestive of a global recession.

> It's
>> all
>>> so
>>>> very
>>>>> exhausting.

But it likely didn't have to be this way! Countries from New Zealand and Taiwan to Germany and Canada have shown how competent political leadership and a strong sense of a collectivist public good can largely halt or at least significantly slow the spread of the coronavirus. But for many of us in the United States, we have been left out on an island—albeit one we have been alone on for quite some time. For as George Packer (2020) wrote, the coronavirus did not break America; *it revealed what was already broken.* As he put it,

> When the virus came here, it found a country with serious underlying conditions, and it exploited them ruthlessly. Chronic ills—a corrupt political class, sclerotic bureaucracy, a heartless economy, a divided and distracted public—had gone untreated for years. [...] The crisis demanded a response that was swift, rational, and collective. The United States reacted instead like Pakistan or Belarus—like a country with shoddy infrastructure and a dysfunctional government whose leaders were too corrupt or too stupid to head off mass suffering.
>
> *(paras 1–2)*

Perhaps it all would have been a bit more manageable and a lot less tragic if we had not had to contend with the most disastrous presidency in modern American memory—one openly bathed in white nationalist rhetoric and scaffolded by the gathering tide of authoritarian politics and policies. (Though perhaps that is a bit of our own magical thinking at work.)

Much has been written about the impact of white nationalism in relation to the Trump administration (see, e.g., Guerrero, 2020; Neiwert, 2017), but what has been less often discussed in mainstream critiques of the last four years is the authoritarian trajectory the Trump administration has sought to compel. In what turned out to be a rather prophetic article, Matthew C. MacWilliams (2016) found during the 2016 Republican presidential primary a "single statistically significant variable [that] predicts whether a voter supports Trump" was not race, income, or education levels but rather one's "authoritarian inclinations" (para 2). Importantly, he wrote on the eve of the 2020 election that while it would continue to flourish if Trump were re-elected, "it won't magically vanish if he loses" (para 5).

Thankfully, by the grace of all that is good and decent in the world, Trump lost his re-election bid. As we write this Introduction (days after the 2020 U.S. Presidential election), Joe Biden is the President-elect; Kamala Harris is the Vice President-elect. There is reason to celebrate, in the way one celebrates a victory over an existential threat to democracy (and, when you consider climate policy, human existence). Political pundits will likely forever ruminate over the what the election results "means", but this much is true: Trump the political actor was soundly defeated as voters turned out in record numbers to reject him, but Trump*ism*—that agglomeration of white nationalism, authoritarianism, science denialism, sexism, racism, homophobia—will not go quietly into the night. For all of Trump's foibles, he didn't create that which has been labeled as Trumpism—he revealed it, was supported by it, and, of course, amplified it—and some *70 million* Americans voted for him in the 2020 election. Even though Biden received roughly 80 million votes—the most votes ever recorded for a U.S. Presidential candidate—the U.S. electoral college made the race for the White House too excruciatingly close for comfort.

Many election post-mortems have touched on and supported the notion that the particular brand of authoritarian populism proffered by Trump is here to stay. Writing in *Foreign Affairs*, Daron Acemoglu (2020) suggests

> this contentious election season should leave no one sanguine about the future. The autocratic, populist turn of the Trump presidency arose from deep fractures in U.S. politics and society, and Americans must understand and address these if they are to prevent similar forces from once again seizing the nation. The roots of Trumpism don't begin or end with Trump or even with American politics—they are closely connected to economic and political currents affecting much of the world.
>
> *(para 2)*

But the particular American form of authoritarianism is worth discussing further. In his research, MacWilliams (2020) identified that

> American authoritarians, compared with non-authoritarians, are more likely to agree that our country should be governed by a strong leader who doesn't have to bother with Congress or elections. They are more likely to support limiting the freedom of the press and agree that the media is the enemy of the people rather than a valuable independent institution. They are also more likely to think the president should have the power to limit the voice and vote of opposition parties, while believing that those who disagree with them are a threat to our country. [...] American

authoritarians fear diversity. They are more likely to agree that increasing racial, religious and ethnic diversity is a clear and present threat to national security. They are more fearful of people of other races, and agree with the statement that "sometimes other groups must be kept in their place."

(paras 10–11)

It is not surprising that Trump tried to govern largely as the authoritarian he sought to project in the 2016 election, albeit a governance that has been checked at various turns by a (somewhat) independent judiciary and his own ineptitude.

In her book *Twilight of Democracy: The Seductive Lure of Authoritarianism*, Anne Applebaum (2020) highlighted most especially the attack on state institutions broadly enjoyed by wannabe authoritarians, using the particular example of contemporary Poland:

The was very little pretense about any of this. The point of all of these changes was not to make the government run better. The point was to make the government more partisan, the courts more pliable, more beholden to the party. [...] in order to justify breaking the law, the party stopped using ordinary political arguments, and began identifying existential enemies instead.

(para 3)

Sound familiar? This is, perhaps, how Trump ended up with millions and millions of Americans supporting "Muslim bans", "border walls", the emptying out of experienced foreign policy experts at the State department, and the invalidation and demonization of scientific research. For the fact remains, 70 million Americans looked at the absolute horror of the last four years and said "Yep, give me four more years of that". *This isn't an aberration; it's a sign of things to come* (especially as Trump and his farrago of enablers have for the last few days been screaming into the airwaves that the election was fixed, there was no possible way for Trump to lose, that Biden will be "illegitimate", and that Trump was not accepting the outcome—as if the Constitution cared about his feelings on the matter). The consequence of this, as Zeynep Tufekci (2020) put it in *The Atlantic*, is hair-raising:

A political nap for a few years probably looks appealing to many who opposed Trump, but the real message of this election is not that Trump lost and Democrats triumphed. It's that a weak and untalented politician lost, while the rest of his party has completely entrenched its power over every other branch of government: the perfect setup for a talented right-wing populist to sweep into office in 2024. And make no mistake: They're all thinking about it.

(para 12)

It's
      all
            been
                 so
                       damn
                              exhausting.

This Volume

Collaborative Futures in Qualitative Inquiry is written within and against the twinned crises of Trump/ism and the COVID-19 pandemic—of trying to make sense of, comment on, and perhaps reveal ways out of the emotional and soul-crushing realities of 2020. The annual International Congress of Qualitative Inquiry (ICQI), at which many of the chapters in this volume were originally to be presented, was cancelled in 2020 due to the pandemic (as, we would hasten to add, were many other conferences). Within academia, many have endeavored to adjust to the new normal of pandemic life in terms of researching, teaching, advising, attending virtual conferences, and so forth. But more than these functional aspects of our profession, many if not most have come to reckon with the kind of work they are doing, how they are doing it, and to what ends they hope such endeavors achieve.

What does research mean during a global pandemic? What does it mean to be an academic in these pandemic times? Although some universities have taken steps to "pause" tenure clocks or provide resources for faculty to move courses online, these are but helpful band-aids on a broader philosophical question. The truth of the matter is that academics—like nearly everyone else in any other profession—are increasingly burned out, depleted, and emotionally drained from charging forward these last 11 months as if everything is okay, as if nothing has changed in the world, as if we should just put our heads down and "get to work". But as June Gruber and colleagues (2020) explained, "Faculty burnout—exacerbated by pandemic-related stressors, absent childcare and school, and unrelenting or even accelerating work expectations from colleagues—poses real and serious risk for mental health challenges of unprecedented scope" (quoted in Flaherty, 2020, para. 4). Gruber and colleagues (2020) further explained

> We have struggled with our own mental and physical well-being—as well as challenges associated with canceled vacations, lack of child care, the illnesses and death of people close to us, and the mental weight of difficult conversations about racial injustices. We've also been worrying about our trainees and the undergraduate students in our classes. The academic and nonacademic job markets have cratered, and some of our colleagues and

students have lost internships and job offers as organizations have been forced to cut expenses. *To be absolutely clear: This. Is. Not. Normal.*

(para 3, our emphases)

We can't keep acting like it's normal. The title of this book privileges the notion of collaboration as front and center to this project. But we are not talking about simply collaborating with another scholar (though we of course see value in that). Rather, we see collaborative inquiry as that which is united in common purpose. Collectively and collaboratively, this moment calls for a critical, performative, social justice inquiry directed at the multiple crises of our historical present. We need a rethinking of where we have been, and, critically, where we are going. We cannot go at it alone. We need to imagine new ways to collaborate, to engage in research and activism. New ways of representing and intervening into the historical present. New ways to conduct research, and a rethinking of in whose interest our research benefits. *That is the mandate of this volume.*

This volume is organized into three sections: (I) Political Futures; (II) Performative Futures; and (III) Global Futures. In Chapter One ("The COVID-19 pandemic is exposing the plague of neoliberalism"), Henry A. Giroux contextualizes the pandemic landscape as one that reaches beyond medical crisis to that of political and ideological crises—one characterized by the hollowing out of public health and the public good, the defunding of institutions that support them, and the celebration of inequality and personal responsibility that privilege and perpetuate the market over all else. We can think here of the calls in some Western countries to rapidly reopen the economy on the basis that sacrificing the health and safety of the public was "worth it" to keep the economy in good working order. But it goes beyond a simple, short-sighted economic responses to the broader organizing force of many countries, but especially the United States, which saw federal responses left languishing or incompetent, a vacuum to be filled (or not) by private interests and crony capitalists with no-bid contracts for personal protective equipment or COVID-19 test. Such actions, Giroux argues, "celebrates death over human life, capital over human needs, greed over compassion, exploitation over justice, and fear over shared responsibilities". Combined with assaults on science, journalists, universities, and popular culture within the Trump era, Giroux sees the pandemic crisis creating "extraordinary circumstances for restricting civil liberties, free speech, and human rights while intensifying the possibilities for an emerging authoritarianism". Our only response, he concludes, must be in reimagining a world in which the future does not mimic the neoliberal present, for otherwise it will continue to repeat and ultimately devour itself.

In Chapter Two ("Becoming weary/wary"), Aaron M. Kuntz examines the practice of "standing vigil" as an extension of engaging with our historical present and the transgressive potential of "confecting anew" within the indeterminate space of "looking out". In his view, "confecting anew" is a process of inquiry; "a making that aims for potential over possibility"—which is especially pressing against the grips of the growing realities of fascism and authoritarianism spanning the globe. To this end, he considers the affective entanglement of weary/wary that produces a "type of exhaustive paralysis" we encounter, especially in pandemic times. His chapter thus stands as both hopeful intervention and cautionary tale for navigating the rough waters collapsing on our shores.

Section II begins with Chapter Three ("Betweeners"), in which Claudio Moreira and Marcelo Diversi write of searching for our common humanity in repressive times. They argue that the global pandemic has both highlighted our shared human vulnerability and global connections and also strengthened our resolve to come together for the sake of survival. Significantly, they cast the struggle to come together as one wrought with ontological, epistemological, and ethical imperatives and implications. Through their poetic voice and verse, Moreira and Diversi look for answers in education, activism, and the spaces of the in-between.

In Chapter Four ("The emotional geographies of academic writing"), Sophie Tamas, Katarina Georgaras, and Maria Dabboussy lead us through an exploration of the emotional work navigated by researchers in pandemic times. In beautifully crafted words, they work through process, anxiety, relationality, trauma—and the spaces of writing that bring these elements to fruition. Specifically, they engage with the foregoing in terms of autoethnography, and how the autoethnographic project can help make sense of the world, the self. As they write, "We need stories when we're afraid".

In Chapter Five ("It is a lonely voice between social rebellion and the pandemic"), César A. Cisneros-Puebla writes about the possibilities of creative subversion and rebellion, especially as related to collective action. He sees creative subversion as a politically-oriented methodological approach to activism, one that has its generative beginnings in the Situationist International movement and Marxist forms of political criticism. Elements of this project include, for example, timely acts of artistic expression, acts of protest and love, and acts that build toward an ecologically sustainable world. To illustrate this project, Cisneros-Puebla turns to the case of Chile during the pandemic and offers "a personal narrative about the Chilean drama of the popular rebellion in its connection with the COVID-19 pandemic from the perspective of love as resistance".

In Chapter Six ("Whimsy, ethnographic writing, and the everyday"), Katie Fitzpatrick and Jonathan Wyatt engage with the notion of the whimsical, which interrupts our focus on the banal, the practical, the instrumental. As they posit, it is the thing out of place: a rose on the pavement, a magnolia inexplicably in full bloom in the winter grey, a bright red velvet coat, a downpour as you're getting out of the car without an umbrella; art slid under a door to say "thank you". In this chapter, they think, write, and play with notions of whimsy, drawing into their scrutiny and inquiry reflections on how whimsy intersects our everyday living and working, and how it applies to ethnographic writing. Engaging with prose and poetic writing both before and during the COVID-19 pandemic, they consider how each of them have been living through the pandemic, and how whimsy offers a way to experience as well as to write. They argue that whimsy is both relational and contextual, as well as political, but that its power lies in the aesthetic and the indirect. Whimsy can be disruptive and powerful, they conclude, but it is a power that asserts itself gently, slowly, even arbitrarily.

Part III begins with Chapter Seven ("Still stumbling toward indigenization, reconciliation, and decolonization"), in which Patrick Lewis both challenges us and charts a way forward for those of us in the academy—especially those with leadership positions or other positions of influence—to subvert the systems and structures of settler colonialism and work toward more impactful forms of reconciliation, indigenization, and decolonization than perhaps have heretofore been realized. To this end, he posits that faculties and departments must take up and recognize Indigenous research and scholarship, not as academic exercise but as a series of policy relations that relate to tenure and promotion processes, work environments, community engagement, and other resources to support Indigenous scholars. In so doing, the historical role of the university as a de-indigenizing force must be reckoned with, including a critique that recent embraces of decolonization by official levers of the university are often more discursive (i.e., recognizing past injustices, land acknowledgment statements) rather than substantive (i.e., financial plans, faculty and student resources, and policy changes), and are often still framed as assimilative (i.e., casting the current culture of the academy at the center of these indigenizing efforts).

In Chapter Eight ("Slow-motion activism"), Magdalena Kazubowski-Houston rethinks the activist potential of performance ethnography, a cross-disciplinary research approach that employs theatre and performance as a form of ethnographic process and/or representation. As she argues, most performance ethnography approaches conceptualize activism if not as a grandiose, vocal, and highly visible action, then at least as an intentional commitment. In contrast, she focuses in this chapter on how performance employed as ethnography can facilitate an activism that works slowly and subtly, creating embodied and affective imaginaries with inadvertent transformative capacities. To do this, she traces how, in a dramatic storytelling project that studied the impact of migration on Polish Romani women's experiences of aging, such activist imaginaries have been staged as performances of impossible futures, bringing together reality, fiction, and human and spirit worlds. As such, Kazubowski-Houston contributes to ongoing transdisciplinary debates on the activist potential of performance ethnography by demonstrating how intimate, performative imaginings of the future can be central players in—not merely passive bystanders of—geopolitical processes.

In Chapter Nine ("Big data, thick data, digital transformation, and the fourth Industrial Revolution"), Julianne Cheek engages with the rise of "data" as a commodity, especially as it relates to the importance of inserting qualitative inquiry "into the digital mix". Using the example of health tracking apps during the pandemic (such as the Australian government's COVIDsafe tracking app), Cheek points to gaps in digital thinking that overlook the social spaces in which such apps exist, and how (and by whom) they are used. The corrective to such outcomes, she suggests, is placing people at the center of digital and technological conversations rather than at the margins where they have historically been relegated. This involves coming to terms with "big data" in research not as simple buzzword but, critically, as the interplay of culture and technology, the role of the researcher in crafting, creating, and interpreting big data, and the societal contexts which allow for, often privilege, and sometimes trouble datafication in the first place.

The volume comes to a close with John M. Johnson's Coda ("Sublime resistance"), in which he outlines a proactive vision of (scholarly) resistance politics and action predicated on transcendent values of peace and personal security; health and wellness; climate change and the environment; love and community.

By Way of a Conclusion

We live in ever-changing, ever more complicated times. The year 2020 has pushed personal and professional lives to the brink, strained an already-strained system far beyond its healthy capacity, and ushered in a growing chorus of dark forces. But at the same time, this year has witnessed the creative, collaborative, and life-affirming resolve of so many in our communities—from political activists and organizers to health-care workers and school teachers, from grocery store and postal delivery service employees to restaurant staff and university faculty. If 2020 has shown us anything, it is that life can change in an instant. We do not know what the social landscape will look like this time next year, or even three months from now. What we do know is that our community of qualitative researchers has a role to play. It is up to you to determine what stories to tell, what spaces to intervene and change, how to ensure the lessons of 2020 are never forgotten. *We have a job to do; let's get to it.*

Notes

1 COVID-19 is an extremely contagious respiratory and vascular disease that causes multiple complications, including bilateral interstitial pneumonia, organ failure, septic shock, blood clots, disorientation, and lingering fatigue and malaise (the lattermost colloquially categorized as "long COVID"). It is caused by the severe acute respiratory syndrome coronavirus, or SARS-CoV-2. As of this writing (November 2020), there have been

50.1 million confirmed cases, and 1.25 million deaths; nearly 20% of all global cases (10 million) and 20% of all deaths (~230,000) have occurred in the United States.
2 We recognize the United States is not the center of the universe, and that the impact of COVID-19 is a global phenomenon experienced differently throughout the world.
3 A survey from the U.S. Centers for Disease Control (CDC) indicated that 4% of respondents "had consumed or gargled diluted bleach solutions" to protect themselves because of Trump's statement that it would be effective (Smith-Schoenwalder, 2020). Trump, it should be pointed out, eventually contracted COVID-19 in October 2020 (as did many senior White House officials). It was widely reported that he was given the drugs dexamethasone and remdesivir, as well as pharmaceutical company Regeneron's monoclonal antibody therapy; no mention of Trump taking hydroxychloroquine was ever publicly stated by a reputable news organization (see Gallagher, 2020).

References

Acemoglu, D. (2020, November 6). Trump won't be the last American populist. *Foreign Affairs.* Retrieved from https://www.foreignaffairs.com/articles/united-states/2020-11-06/trump-wont-be-last-american-populist

Applebaum, A. (2020). *Twilight of democracy: The seductive lure of authoritarianism.* New York: Doubleday.

Flaherty, C. (2020, September 14). Burning out. *Inside Higher Ed.* Retrieved from https://www.insidehighered.com/news/2020/09/14/faculty-members-struggle-burnout

Gallagher, J. (2020, October 9). Dexamethasone, remdesivir, Regeneron: Trump's Covid treatment explained. *BBC.* Retrieved from https://www.bbc.com/news/health-54418464

Greenhalgh, T. (2020). Face coverings for the public: Laying straw men to rest. *Journal of Evaluation in Clinical Practice.* Retrieved from https://doi.org/10.1111/jep.13415

Greenhalgh, T., Schmid, M. B., Czypioonka, T., Bassler, D., & Gruer, L. (2020). Face masks for the public during the covid-10 crisis. *The BMJ.* Retrieved from https://www.bmj.com/content/369/bmj.m1435

Gruber, J., Van Bavel, J. J., Cunningham, W. A., Somerville, L. H., & Lewis, Jr., N. A. (2020, August 28). Academia needs a reality: Life is not back to normal. *Science.* Retrieved from https://www.sciencemag.org/careers/2020/08/academia-needs-reality-check-life-not-back-normal

Guerrero, J. (2020). *Hatemonger: Stephen Miller, Donald Trump and the white nationalist agenda.* New York: William Morrow.

Holtgrave, D., Barranco, M. A., Tesoriero, J. M., Blog, D. S., Rosenberg, E. S. (2020). Assessing racial and ethnic disparities using a COVID-19 outcomes continuum for New York State. *Annals of Epidemiology, 48,* 9–14.

Long, H. (2020, April 16). U.S. now has 22 million unemployed, wiping out a decade of job gains. *The Washington Post.* Retrieved from https://www.washingtonpost.com/business/2020/04/16/unemployment-claims-coronavirus/

MacWilliams, M. C. (2016). The one weird trait that predicts whether you're a Trump supporter. *Politico.* Retrieved from https://www.politico.com/magazine/story/2016/01/donald-trump-2016-authoritarian-213533

MacWilliams, M. C. (2020). Trump is an authoritarian; so are millions of Americans. *Politico.* Retrieved from https://www.politico.com/news/magazine/2020/09/23/trump-america-authoritarianism-420681

Neiwert, D. (2017). *Alt-America: The rise of the radical right in the age of Trump.* New York: Verso.

Packer, G. (2020). We are living in a failed state. *The Atlantic.* Retrieved from https://www. theatlantic.com/magazine/archive/2020/06/underlying-conditions/610261/

Patton, M. (2020, October 12). The impact of COVID-19 on U.S. economy and financial markets. *Forbes.* Retrieved from https://www.forbes.com/sites/mikepatton/2020/10/12/ the-impact-of-covid-19-on-us-economy-and-financial-markets

Smith-Schoenwalder, C. (2020, June 5). CDC: Some people did take bleach to protect from coronavirus. *US News & World Report.* Retrieved from https://www.usnews. com/news/health-news/articles/2020-06-05/cdc-some-people-did-take-bleach-to-protect-from-coronavirus

Tufekci, Z. (2020, November 6). America's next authoritarian will be much more competent. *The Atlantic.* Retrieved from https://www.theatlantic.com/ideas/archive/2020/11/ trump-proved-authoritarians-can-get-elected-america/617023/

SECTION I
Political Futures

1

THE COVID-19 PANDEMIC IS EXPOSING THE PLAGUE OF NEOLIBERALISM[1]

Henry A. Giroux

The current coronavirus pandemic is more than a medical crisis—it is also a political and ideological crisis. It is a crisis deeply rooted in years of neglect by neoliberal governments that denied the importance of public health and the public good while defunding the institutions that made them possible. At the same time, this crisis cannot be separated from the crisis of massive inequalities in wealth, income and power. Nor can it be separated from a crisis of democratic values, education and environmental destruction.

The coronavirus pandemic is deeply interconnected with the politicization of the natural order through its destructive assaults waged by neoliberal globalization on the ecosystem (Leven & Overwijk, 2020). In addition, it cannot be disconnected from the spectacle of racism, ultra-nationalism, anti-immigrant sentiment and bigotry that has dominated the national zeitgeist as a means of promoting shared fears rather than shared responsibilities. The plague has as one of its roots a politics of depoliticization, which makes clear that education is a central feature of politics, and it always plays a central role—whether in a visible or a veiled way—in any ideological project. For instance, it has been a central pedagogical principle of neoliberalism that individual responsibility is the only way to address social problems, and consequently, there is no need to address broader systemic issues, hold power accountable or embrace matters of collective responsibility. As a politics of containment, neoliberalism privatizes and individualizes social problems, i.e., wash your hands as a way to contain the pandemic. In doing so, cultural critics Bram Leven and Jan Overwijk (2020) argue, "it seeks to contain any real democratic politics; that is to say, a politics based on collective solidarity and equality [because] democratic politics is a threat to the market" (para. 18).

Additionally, neoliberalism's emphasis on commercial values rather than democratic values, its virulent ideology of extreme competitiveness, irrational selfishness and its impatience with matters of ethics, justice and truth has undermined critical thought and the power of informed judgment. As Pankaj Mishra (2020) states, "for decades now, de-industrialization, the outsourcing of jobs, and then automation, have deprived many working people of their security and dignity, making the aggrieved…vulnerable to demagoguery" (para. 15).

Americans live in an age when neoliberalism wages war on the public and inequality is recast as a virtue. This age supports notions of individual responsibility that tear up social solidarities in devastating ways. This is a historical moment that puts a premium on competitive attitudes and unchecked individualism, and allows the market to become a template for structuring all social relations. The social contract has been all but eliminated while notions of the public good, social obligations and democratic forms of solidarity are under attack. This is a form of gangster capitalism that speaks only in the market-based language of profits, privatization and commercial exchange. It also legitimates the language of isolation, deprivation, human suffering and death.

Ravaged for decades by neoliberal policies, American society is plagued by a series of crises whose deeper roots have intensified the stark class and racial divides. Such a divide in evident in the millions of workers who do not have paid sick leave, the millions who lack health insurance, the hundreds of thousands who are homeless, and the fact that "One in five Americans cannot pay their bills on time and 40 percent do not have the savings needed to cover an unexpected \$400 expense" (Kapczynski & Gonsalves, 2020, para. 12). Neoliberal capitalism is the underlying pandemic feeding the current global shortage of hospitals, medical supplies, beds and robust social welfare provisions, and increasingly an indifference to human life.

Under such circumstances, the social sphere and its interconnections become an object of either financial exploitation or utter disdain, or both. What is lost in this depoliticizing discourse of neoliberalism and made clear in the current pandemic is that our lives are indeed interconnected for better or worse. There is a certain irony here in that the current White House call for the public to abide by social distancing mirrors not only a medically safe practice to slow down the spread of the virus, but it also occupies a long-standing neoliberal ideological space that disdains social connections and democratic values while promoting death-dealing forms of social atomization. Here is where the medical crisis runs head on into a long-standing political crisis. This is also the space where politics has become a tool of neoliberalism as the economy and powers of government relentlessly attack and erode the common good and democracy itself. Irony turns into moral and political irresponsibility as Trump pushes social distancing while also indicating he will relax social distancing guidelines, against the advice of public health experts, in order to reboot the economy.

In a time of crisis, capitalism reveals itself as a disimagination machine whose underlying message is that the market provides the only forms of agency left. In this context, political, economic and social forces become the new workstations incessantly pushing the flight from any vestige of social, ethical and political responsibility, parading as the new common sense. Politics becomes a war machine running overtime to habituate people to the abyss of power while undermining any sense of dissent, resistance and social justice. Of course, this is the wider context of neoliberalism in which the coronavirus pandemic operates.

The financial crisis of 2008 made visible the plague of neoliberalism that has for over 40 years ravaged the public good and imposed misery and suffering upon the poor and others considered excess, waste or dangerous. With its merging of brutal austerity policies, financialization of the economy, the concentration of power in few hands and the language of racial and social cleansing, neoliberalism has morphed into a form of fascist politics. The new political formation is characterized by a distinctive and all-embracing politics of disposability, a massive gutting of the social state, and support for pedagogical apparatuses of spectacularized violence, fear mongering and state terror.

All of which point to a disdain for any notion of the social that expands the meaning and possibilities of the common good, including the crucial sphere of public health, and the broader notion of how what Michael Sandel calls "living together in a community" (quoted in Friedman, 2020, para. 6), in which matters of solidarity and the sacrifices we make function to treat people with compassion, humanity and dignity. Central to this notion of the common good, argues Shai Lavi (2009), is a mass movement willing to bring together struggles for emancipation, economic justice and political community established on the basis of human equality.

The brutality of the pandemic of neoliberalism is evident in Trump's call on March 16, 2020 to "reopen the economy," by Easter. At that time, he wanted to move the United States quickly toward ending cautious measures such as social distancing and letting the virus run its course. Trump's initial rational for such an action restated a right-wing argument that "the cure is worse than the disease." After being told that 2.2 million people could die as a result of reopening the economy too early, Trump said the White House will keep its guidelines for social distancing in place through the end of April (see Samuels & Chalfant, 2020).

Dr. Anthony Fauci, the Director of the National Institute of Allergy and Infectious Diseases, has stated that social distancing is the most important tool for containing the virus, yet, Trump still refuses to issue a national stay at home order, especially at a time when eight states do not have one. At a press conference on April 4, Trump had stated that things will get a lot worse with many more deaths. Yet, soon afterwards, he reiterated that he would like to see the country open again. Such actions display a shocking level of moral turpitude, making clear that Trump is more concerned about his reelection, commerce and the stock market than the ensuing death toll. As Robert Costa and Philip Rucker (2020) wrote in the *Washington Post*, "Trump has long viewed the stock market as a barometer for his own reelection hopes" (para. 4).

The not-so-hidden and terrifying message is that political opportunism, the drive for profits and the embrace of a cruel neoliberal ideology are being embraced by the Trump administration without apology. Trump appears to take pleasure in belittling experts and expertise and only follows the advice of public health officials in the midst of the most dire warnings. He treats the pandemic as a partisan battle, disparages governors desperately calling for supplies and refuses to implement a coordinated national federal approach to addressing the crisis.

Without hard evidence or scientific proof, Trump endorses specific drugs as treatments, falsely claims the United States is close to a vaccine, and often relies on the advice of right-wing pundits who push conspiracy theories. When it comes to the choice of saving lives or the economy, Trump appears more concerned about the fate of Wall Street. What is more, his often confused and contradictory public remarks are filled with hyperbole and falsehoods and serve to mislead the American public while potentially causing unimaginable misery along with the possibility that "Tens of thousands, perhaps millions would get sick and die" (Cohen, 2020, para. 4). In this instance, sheer incompetence coupled with an aversion to experts and scientific evidence rise to the status of being a public danger and a catastrophic crisis.

In light of the ongoing spread of deaths, infections and hospital shortages and public health catastrophe, experts have called for long-term planning strategies, increased testing and coordination between the federal government and the states (see Wan, 2020). Many Governors have complained that the government's lack of a federal plan has created something akin of the wild west—"a system beset by shortages, inefficiencies and disorder" (Stanley-Becker, 2020).

The urgency of demands are amplified by the fact that the White House and leadership at multiple levels failed to provide any sense of urgency and immediacy in the early stage of the looming crisis (see, e.g., Shear et al. 2020). Additionally, a report in *The Washington Post* stated that it took Trump 70 days from first being notified about the grave implications of the coronavirus to treat it "not as a distant threat or harmless flu strain well under control, but as a lethal force that had outflanked America's defenses and was poised to kill tens of thousands of citizens" (Abutaleb, Dawsey, Nakashima, & Miller, 2020).

Of course, the many people who are and will die as a result of this reckless policy will be those traditionally viewed as disposable under the reign of neoliberalism. These include the elderly, the destitute, poor people of color, undocumented immigrants and people with disabilities—not to mention the frontline medical workers who lack the equipment they need to be safe as they treat the elderly, sick and dangerously ill.

There is more at work here than a hardened depravity of an ill-informed, petty celebrity politician who is causing havoc and needless human suffering in a time of crisis. Trump has always had a penchant for thoughtlessness and self-absorption, and takes delight in humiliating others. Citing Stephen Greenblatt (2018) in a different context, his words perfectly fit Trump for whom "There is no deep secret about his cynicism, cruelty and treacherousness, no glimpse of anything redeemable in him, and no reason to believe that he could ever govern the country effectively" (para. 12).

Trump's crudeness, mendacity, disregard for science and arbitrary rule had led him to disregard previous warnings from experts about the possibility of a looming pandemic. This willful form of ignorance and sheer effrontery was on display in his earlier refusal and colossal failure to mobilize the power of the federal government to provide widespread testing and masks while simultaneously ensuring that hospitals and medical staff had enough beds, masks, ventilators and other personal protective equipment for treating people infected with the virus.

Ed Pilkington and Tom McCarthy (2020) report in *The Guardian* that Trump not only downplayed the threat the virus posed after the first case appeared on January 20, but his actions were "mired in chaos and confusion" (para. 4). Rather than act quickly to avert a national health disaster, Trump let six weeks go by before his administration took seriously the severity of the threat and the need for mass testing. In their article, Pilkington and McCarthy quote Jeremy Konyndyk, who led the U.S. government's response in 2013–2017 to a number of international disasters. He stated: "We are witnessing in the United States one of the greatest failures of basic governance and basic leadership in modern times" (para. 15).

Trump has a penchant for turning politics in a form of theater and entertainment in a form of cruelty. In a shocking display of pettiness, he publicly told Vice President Mike Pence not to answer the calls of those governors who are not "appreciative" of his efforts to deal with the pandemic (see Wilkie & Breuninger, 2020). This includes Washington Governor Jay Inslee and Michigan Governor Gretchen Whitmer, both of whom have made desperate pleas for critically needed supplies.

Moreover, as part of an ongoing effort to shift blame away from himself, Trump has attacked and attempted to humiliate reporters who asked him critical questions, and went so far as to claim that "hospitals had squandered or done worse with masks and were 'hoarding' ventilators, and that states were requesting equipment despite not needing them." He went so far as to suggest that much needed masks were "going out the backdoor" (Blake, 2020, para. 3). It is hard to overlook this type of weaponized cruelty, especially given the moving pleas by medical professionals appearing on social media begging for masks, gowns, ventilators and other crucial protective and lifesaving equipment. There is more at work here than the politics of denial and solipsism on the part of Trump; there is also what Robert Jay Lifton (2019) calls "malignant normality," which I interpret as behavior that revels in violence and is fueled by what appears to be an immense pleasure in engaging in acts of cruelty. We have seen echoes of such cruelty in other eras with consequences that resulted in the death of millions, such as in the lynching of African-Americans in the United States and acts of genocide in Nazi Germany.

Trump's obsession with wealth and ratings, and his limitless self-regard define him not only as an inept leader but also as a dangerous fraud. For instance, in the midst of the rapidly rising death toll in the United States, Trump boasted at one of his press media appearances "about the [high] ratings for the White House's coronavirus task force briefings" (quoted in Stetler, 2020). This is a form of political theater and pandemic pedagogy that weaponizes a rising death toll and in the service of entertainment. Trump's incompetence bears tragic results in that hospitals are overcrowded, medical personal lacking adequate protective equipment are dying and the governors of hardest-hit states such as New York appear to be in a running feud with Trump, who is more at ease in insulting governors who have criticized him for his lack of leadership than in supplying them with much-needed medical equipment.

Trump and his administration are not alone in pushing a necropolitics that celebrates death over life, capital over human needs, greed over compassion, exploitation over justice and fear over shared responsibilities. How else to explain the chorus of Trump's supporters in the media, corporate board rooms and the White House arguing for rationing life-saving care on the basis of age and dis- ability in order to prevent imposing drastic strains on the nation's hospitals and the U.S. economy? How else to explain that long before this pandemic crisis, as Naomi Klein (2017) points out, the apostles of neoliberalism have attempted to underfund services such as "state-funded health care, clean water, good public schools, safe workplaces, pensions, and other programs to care for the elderly and disadvantaged." At the same time, she continues, a war has been waged by predatory capitalism on "the very idea of the public sphere and the public good." One consequence is that "the publicly owned bones of society—roads, bridges, levees and water systems—are going to slip into a state of such disrepair that it takes little to push them beyond the breaking point. When you massively cut taxes so that you don't have money to spend on much of anything besides the police and the military, this is what happens."

What is being revealed in the current pandemic crisis is the underlying plague of neoliberalism that has dominated the global economy for the last 40 years, though increasingly brandished as a badge of honor by fascist politicians such as Trump, Brazilian President Jair Bolsonaro, Indian Prime Minister Narendra Modi and others. Ruling-class corruption is also readily visible in a bailout package which, as Rob Urie (2020) observes, amounts to "Bailouts for the rich, the virus for the rest of us" (para. 1). He writes:

> In an economy where the richest 1% takes all the gains while the poor and working class haven't seen a raise in four decades, it is the rich who will reap the benefits while workers get sick and die. It is finance capitalism that is being bailed out when it should have suffocated under its own weight in 2009.
>
> *(Para 2)*

What is being revealed in this looming pandemic is an unabashed resurgence of fascist politics with its history of grotesque inequalities, disposability, unadulterated cruelty and regressive policies. The latter neoliberal rudiments have a long legacy in the United States and have returned with revenge under the Trump administration. Neoliberal fascism signals a resurgence of a terror that bears an eerie echo to the racial cleansing and embrace of eugenics that marked the purification policies of the Hitler regime and made the concentration camp the endpoint of fascism. This was also policy designed to reboot the economy in a time of crisis.

We live at a time of multiple plagues that fuel the current coronavirus epidemic that is engulfing the globe inflicting economic misery, suffering and death as they move through societies with the speed of a deadly tornado. These include the plague of ecological destruction, the degradation of civic culture, the possibility of a nuclear war and the normalization of a brutal culture of cruelty. Moreover, the plague of neoliberalism has waged a full-scale attack on the welfare state. In doing so, it has underfunded and weakened those institutions such as education and the public health sector. In addition, it has removed the vast majority of Americans from the power relations and modes of governance that would enable them to deal critically and intelligently with natural disasters, pandemics and a slew of planetary crises which cannot be addressed by the market. In the midst of this pandemic, the poison of ruling-class power is at the center of the current political, ideological and medical crisis. Frank Rich (2020) got it right in arguing:

> ...the pandemic has revealed in particularly stark terms that the extreme economic inequalities unmasked by the 2008 economic collapse remain unaddressed. There's a titanic dynamic playing out now in real time. Celebrities and the wealthy are first in line for the lifeboats of coronavirus tests. Rupert Murdoch and his family protect their own health while profiting from a news empire that downplayed and outright disputed the threat of coronavirus…. As the virus spreads from its current epicenters through the country the grotesque discrepancy between the elites and the have-nots is going to make *Parasite* look as benign as an episode of *Modern Family*.

The other plague, among many, is the rise of right-wing cultural apparatuses such as *Fox News* and Breitbart Media in which truth is treated with scorn, science viewed as a hindrance and critical thought is maligned as "fake news." This is a plague of willful ignorance and state-sanctioned civic illiteracy.

Under such circumstances, language at the highest levels of power and among powerful conservative cultural apparatuses operates in the service of denial, lies and violence. These media relentlessly push conspiracy theories such as the claim that the pandemic is a product of the "deep state" designed to prevent Trump from being reelected; a hoax created by the Democratic Party; or a virus that is no less dangerous than the common flu. They have also relentlessly insisted that all social problems are a matter of individual responsibility so as to depoliticize the public while making them indifferent to the neofascist claim that the government has no responsibility to care for its citizens or that society should not be organized around mutual respect, care, social rights and economic equality.

The current crisis is part of an age defined by a pedagogical catastrophe of indifference and a flight from any viable sense of moral responsibility. This is an age marked by a contempt for weakness, as well as rampant racism, the elevation of emotion over reason, the collapse of civic culture and an obsession with wealth and self-interest. Under such circumstances, we are in the midst of not simply a political crisis, but also an educational crisis in which matters of power, governance, knowledge and a disdain for truth and evidence have wreaked havoc on the truth and endangered both millions of people and the planet itself. This is a politics fueled by a disimagination machine whose political and cultural workstations make the truth, justice, ethics and, most of all, bodies disappear into the abyss of authoritarianism.

For the plague to end, it is crucial to address the ideologies of neoliberal fascism that prevent people from translating private troubles into broader systemic issues and to fight pedagogically in order convince the public to move beyond the culture of privatization and atomization that propels a consumer society and reinforces a politics of single issues detached from broader considerations. This political crisis can only be grasped as a crisis of the social totality, one in which a range of "democratic ills form the specifically political strand of a general crisis that is engulfing our social order in its entirety" (Fraser, 2018, para. 2). We live in a moment in which it is becoming more credible to acknowledge that capitalism and democracy are not the same thing, and that the endpoint of capitalism is not only massive inequality and human suffering but a brutal machinery of death in which humanity is one step closer to the edge of extinction. This suggests that crises can have multiple outcomes resulting in a surge of authoritarianism and repression, on the one hand; or on the other, a resurgence of resistance movements at numerous levels willing to fight for a more just and equitable society, one that rejects what Brad Evans has called an age of multiple exclusions, mass terror, increasing expulsions and the hollowing out of the social state.

The coronavirus pandemic has pulled back the curtain to reveal the power of a brutal neoliberalism—and its global financial markets—in all of its cruelty. This is a system that has not only eroded the democratic ideals of equality and popular sovereignty but has also created a political and economic context in which the looming pandemic puts a severe strain on medical workers and hospitals that lack ventilators and other essential equipment to treat patients and limit the number of deaths caused by the virus. This points to a moment in the current historical conjuncture in which the space between the passing of one period and the beginning of a new age offers the possibility for the social and political imagination to set in motion a global movement for radical democracy.

The current viral pandemic cannot be discussed outside of the crisis of politics and education. What is needed is a new vocabulary to comprehend the current pandemic crisis. Such a language must provide a sustained critique of neoliberal fascism with its discourses of exclusion, exploitation and racial purity. Such a discourse should also address the underlying causes of poverty, class domination, environmental destruction and a resurgent racism not as a call for reform, but as a project of radical reconstruction aimed at the creation of a new political and economic social order. In the words of Amartya Sen, we need "to think big about society" (quoted in Markandeya & Layak, 2011, para. 7). In spite of the overwhelming nature of the current crisis, there is a need to think beyond being isolated, overwhelmed and powerless.

As we have seen in a number of countries such as Hungary, Egypt, the Philippines, Thailand and Israel, the pandemic crisis creates extraordinary circumstances for restricting civil liberties, free speech and human rights while intensifying the possibilities of an emerging authoritarianism. There is no doubt that the Covid-19 crisis will test the limits of democracy worldwide.

At the same time, the magnitude of the crisis offers new possibilities in which people can begin to rethink what kind of society, world and future they want to inhabit. What we do not want to do is to go back to a system that equates democracy and capitalism. We must move beyond the modifying the system, because the current crisis has deeper political and economic roots and demands a complete restructuring of society. David Harvey (2016) is right in arguing that "The fundamental problems are actually so deep right now that there is no way that we are going to go anywhere without a very strong anti-capitalist movement."

As the pandemic crisis recedes, we will have to choose between a society that addresses human needs or one in which a survival-of-the-fittest–ethos and war-of-all against-all becomes the only organizing principle of society. It is time for new visions, public transcripts and pedagogical narratives to emerge about the meaning of politics, solidarity, mass resistance and democracy itself. We still have the opportunity to reimagine a world in which the future does not mimic the predatory neoliberal present. This should be a world which brings together the struggles for justice, emancipation and social equality. More urgent than ever is the need to struggle for a world that imagines and acts on the utopian promises of a just and democratic socialist society. In the face of the Covid-19 pandemic, matters of criticism, understanding and resistance are elevated into a matter of life or death. Resistance is no longer an option; it is a dire necessity.

Note

1 This chapter originally appeared in *Truthout* (https://truthout.org/articles/the-covid-19-pandemic-is-exposing-the-plague-of-neoliberalism/). It is reprinted here by permission of the author.

References

Abutaleb, Y., Dawsey, J., Nakashima, E., & Miller, G. (2020, April 4). The U.S. was beset by denial and dysfunction as the coronavirus raged. *The Washington Post*. Retrieved from https://www.washingtonpost.com/national-security/2020/04/04/coronavirus-government-dysfunction/?arc404=true

Blake, A. (2020, March 29). Trump blames hospitals for mask and ventilator shortage. *The Washington Post*. Retrieved from https://www.washingtonpost.com/politics/2020/03/29/trump-bizarrely-blames-hospitals-mask-ventilator-shortages/

Cohen, M. (2020, March 26). Marching into the abyss. *Boston Globe*. Retrieved from http://view.email.bostonglobe.com/?qs=76c8773b3c83e1ce3706b6e0cd228fbb42be7417c3e64dec72b8a6775015a964e483cdd599d0e4ca541070bc08ad8ed08fef4a6f627574934c2d2815e3c9ea62c1b6dd7a01b6696c324120d3b44768c1a386b19ca7a79c93.

Costa, R., & Rucker, P. (2020). Inside Trump's risky push to reopen the country amid the coronavirus crisis. *The Washington Post*. Retrieved from https://www.washingtonpost.com/politics/inside-trumps-risky-push-to-reopen-the-country-amid-the-coronavirus-crisis/2020/03/28/b87fff62-6ee2-11ea-a3ec-70d7479d83f0_story.html

Fraser, N. (2018). *Democracy's crisis: On the political contradiction of financialized capitalism*. Samuel L. and Elizabeth Jodidi Lecture. Weatherhead Center for International Affairs, Harvard University. Retrieved from https://wcfia.harvard.edu/publications/centerpiece/fall2018/transcript_jodidi11-5-2018

Friedman, T. L. (2020, March 24). Finding the 'common good' in a pandemic: The Harvard political philosopher offers his take. *The New York Times*. Retrieved from https://www.nytimes.com/2020/03/24/opinion/covid-ethics-politics.html

Greenblatt, S. (2018). The tyrant and his enablers. *Longreads*. Retrieved from https://longreads.com/2018/07/18/the-tyrant-and-his-enablers/

Harvey, D. (2016). Neoliberalism is a political project: An interview with David Harvey. *Jacobin Magazine* (Interview by Bjarke Skaerlund Risager). Retrieved from https://www.jacobinmag.com/2016/07/david-harvey-neoliberalism-capitalism-labor-crisis-resistance/

Kapczynski, A., & Gonsalves, G. (2020, March 13). Alone against the virus. *Boston Review*. Retrieved from https://bostonreview.net/class-inequality-science-nature/amy-kapczynski-gregg-gonsalves-alone-against-virus

Klein, N. (2017). *No is not enough: Resisting Trump's shock politics and winning the world we need.* Chicago, IL: Haymarket.

Lavi, S. (2009). Crimes of action, crimes of thought: Arendt on reconciliations, forgiveness, and judgment. In R. Berkowitz, J. Katz, & T. Keenan (Eds.), *Thinking in dark times: Hannah Arendt on ethics and politics* (pp. 229–236). Chicago, IL: Fordham University Press.

Leven, B., & Overwijk, J. (2020, March 23). We created this beast: The political ecology of COVID-19. *EuroZine.* Retrieved from https://www.eurozine.com/we-created-this-beast/

Lifton, R. J. (2019). *Losing reality: on cults, cultism, and the mindset of political and religious zealotry.* Boston, MA: The New Press.

Markandeya, V., & Layak, S. (2011, February 20). Private enterprise needs to think big about society: Amartya Sen. *Business Today* (India). Retrieved from https://www.businesstoday.in/magazine/opinion/interviews/amartya-sen-in-an-exclusive-interview-says-private-enterprise-needs-to-think-big-about-society/story/12905.html

Mishra, P. (2020, March 16). Get ready, a bigger disruption is coming. *Bloomberg.* Retrieved from https://www.bloomberg.com/opinion/articles/2020-03-16/coronavirus-foreshadows-bigger-disruptions-in-future

Pilkington, E., & McCarthy, T. (2020, March 31). The missing six weeks: How Trump failed the biggest test of his life. *The Guardian* (UK). Retrieved from https://www.theguardian.com/us-news/2020/mar/28/trump-coronavirus-politics-us-health-disaster

Rich, F. (2020, March 26). What a plague reveals. *New York Magazine.* Retrieved from https://nymag.com/intelligencer/2020/03/frank-rich-what-a-plague-reveals.html

Samuels, B., & Chalfant, M. (2020, March 29). Trump shifts, says social distancing to go to April 30. *The Hill.* Retrieved from https://thehill.com/homenews/administration/490089-trump-says-social-distancing-guidelines-to-continue-through-end-of

Shear, M. D., Goodnough, A., Kaplan, S., Fink, S., Thomas, K., & Weiland, N. (2020, March 28). The lost month: How a failure to test blinded the U.S. to Covid-10. *The New York Times.* Retrieved from https://www.nytimes.com/2020/03/28/us/testing-coronavirus-pandemic.html

Stanley-Becker, I. (2020, March 31). Governors plead for medical equipment from federal stockpile plagued by shortages and confusion. *The Washington Post.* Retrieved from https://www.washingtonpost.com/politics/governors-plead-for-medical-equipment-from-federal-stockpile-plagued-by-shortages-and-confusion/2020/03/31/18aadda0-728d-11ea-87da-77a8136c1a6d_story.html

Stetler, B. (2020, March 29). As coronavirus death toll rises, Trump focuses on a different set of numbers: TV ratings. *CNN.* Retrieved from https://www.cnn.com/2020/03/29/media/donald-trump-tv-ratings-reliable-sources/index.html

Urie, R. (2020, March 27). Bailouts for the rich, the virus for the rest of us. *CounterPunch.* Retrieved from https://www.counterpunch.org/2020/03/27/bailouts-for-the-rich-the-virus-for-the-rest-of-us/

Wan, W. (2020). Experts converge on plans for easing coronavirus restrictions safely. *The Washington Post.* Retrieved from https://www.washingtonpost.com/health/2020/03/29/coronavirus-strategy-economy-plan

Wilkie, C., & Breuninger, K. (2020, March 27). Trump says he told Pence not to call governors who aren't 'appreciative' of White House coronavirus efforts. *CNBC.* Retrieved from https://www.cnbc.com/2020/03/27/coronavirus-trump-told-pence-not-to-call-washington-michigan-governors.html

2

BECOMING WEARY/WARY: CONFECTING ANEW IN A FASCIST WORLD

Aaron M. Kuntz

As I write this my country is on fire. The literal flames (forest fires) on the West Coast of the United States entangle with political flames (incendiary governmental incompetence and violence) and a health emergency (pandemic) that breed a type of weary/wary exhaustion: gazing about for the next flare up even as one feels the pained imprint of the previous. All of these fires are material, of course, and they mark themselves disproportionally on marginalized and exploited groups with devastating efficiency. Further, these fires are not new; they simply coincide in our contemporary moment in unique ways, producing constellations of meaning—flashpoints—that challenge anew. Similarly, the weary/wary exhaustion that comes with being marked by such explosive circumstance is not new: some groups just have had the opportunity to opt out, if even for a moment; to pause the onslaught and catch one's breath. This opting out is the very articulation of privilege, of course, and it is the normalized order of our contemporary moment that allows some this advantaged placement (of breath, of pause) while refusing others. And the fires rage on.

There are multiple processes and relations that bind us in these trying circumstances (such is the imminent and entangled nature of our shared world) even as there exist an endless array of responses or engagements to such tragedy. In this chapter, I examine the practice of standing vigil as an extension of engaging with our time (sometimes usefully productive, sometimes not) and the transgressive potential of confecting anew within the indeterminate space of "looking out." To my mind, "confecting anew" is a process of inquiry; a making that aims for potential over possibility. Contextually, I set such practices within the animating realities of fascism, a force that fuels the flames of inequity and exploitation; a type of ontopower that has a constitutive effect on the sense of what is possible given our circumstances. In the end, I suppose I pursue a question: "what does it mean to inquire, in this moment, when the world seems perpetually afire?"

Organizationally, I begin this chapter by considering an entangled affect of weary/wary that seems to extend from our contemporary moment—one that draws from processes of late capitalism to often produce a type of exhaustive paralysis that is relentless in its force. Yet, the weary/wary tangle is never definite, never fully exhausted, and so I next turn to practices of standing vigil as a means to engage the potential of indeterminacy. I thus offer Foucault's explication of the vigil as dwelling within indeterminacy, a resistive process through which new alternatives to the status quo are both necessary and inevitable; never exhausted or exhaustible.

Yet no practices are inherently revolutionary or inevitably challenging to the exploitative world order. Consequently, after offering a consideration of the vigil as a potentially transgressive practice, I turn to consider the ease with which participating as a "look out" for various transgressions merges into conservative practices of maintenance, replicating the exploitative status quo. In order to challenge such reductive possibility, I end through offering philosophical inquiry as a means to confect anew through virtuous practices of relational endurance and conceptual creation that refuse the normalizing tendencies of fascisms (overt and subtle). Philosophical inquiry might productively articulate as a practice of standing vigil, confecting anew amidst an indeterminate space of becoming transgressive.

Thus it is that I understand processes of making-anew as a means to articulate a transgressive orientation through the work of inquiry. This is, perhaps, to put to use the weary/wary exhaustion that is an effect of living within a fascist world that violently asserts there is no otherwise. And so we stand vigil, practicing the potential to become differently than we currently are; a challenge to what is because we can no longer bear to be this way, in these times, according to these possibilities that frame our governance. Perhaps through our inquiry processes we might confect anew and, in doing so, become differently than we have been (or will be).

Weary/Wary

Given the circumstances of our world, I have been thinking quite a bit about exhaustion—the moment when one is not fully spent and yet, perhaps, feels the nearing end of possibility. Exhausted, one doesn't stop, but, instead, feels that stopping must soon come. We become exhausted. As Deleuze examines with Parnet (1996), exhaustion resides in the model of the alcoholic's second to last drink, coming before the terminal conclusion of the last. Exhaustion is the penultimate—not final, but pointing to potential loss (not a firm conclusion, but the beginning of the end).

As the second-to-last, exhaustion is oddly productive—generative of something that has not yet come to be. For me, this certainly plays out in my work with inquiry. I wonder about practicing inquiry in these times and I feel a doubled sense of becoming exhausted: pushed to the brink by current events and frustrated by the endless array of methodological techniques built with the intent of ordering what could never be ordered; categorizing to a halt the entangled flows of living. I am weary of the incessant production of such activities and wary of their normalizing possibility. Becoming exhausted by it all. And so I wonder if we might dwell within a degree of methodological exhaustion—a pausing, not yet extinguished but very nearly out-of-gas. At times, I feel a methodological exhaustion as I forever fail to fully keep apace with the potential of our practice, the unyielding presentation of ordering, of technique. And I cannot always answer the question of, "how are we to inquire in a world burning with the imposed violence of inequity and exploitation?" The force of such entangled circumstance nearly claims me and I am spent.

Yet, how might this methodological exhaustion be something more than just an affect of here-we-nearly-conclude? This is, after all, a space of incompletion (exhaustion never concludes). Might this never-done, the blurred edges that mark a potential, provide a singularity of immanent intransigent space? After all, I don't know what to do with exhaustion other than to dwell within it, to feel it. And that lack of direction, of course, does away with the possible upon which method often operates. Exhausted by and within ambiguity. And then the reality of our present moment rushes back in and the felt state of disorientation continues. If this contemporary moment will never conclude (despite, perhaps, our exhausted state) must it then be transformed? What practices must be enacted to ethically orient such change? And how might our work of inquiry be a part of such work, an animating force for potential transformation? And I once again return to the vagaries of our contemporary moment.

Does one ever come to grips with the degrees of violence, exploitation and indignity that extend from living amidst a state that so overtly wields white supremacy as its dominant logic of governance? Can one ever fully refuse the demands of acquiesce, regimentation and forced suppression that articulate in micro and macro forms in these fascist times? The incessant need to *come to grips with* and *refuse* is exhausting, it seems. And, of course, exhaustion articulates as both an affective state and a series of practices that coincide with a system of logics, some dominant and others resistive.

Both acts of *coming to grips with* and *refusing* depend to an extent on recognition. One locates that which is to be understood, even refused. Yet, this seemingly simple act of recognition itself begets exhaustion. This perhaps extends from the ever-present violence that goes hand-in-hand with recognition. Such violence occurs on macro (e.g., the forceful suppression and vicious disruption of peaceful protests) and micro levels (e.g., the erasure of individual identity).

Trying to take in the dynamic and nuanced fascist processes of our contemporary time saps even the most energetic of resistance. This is, of course, because there is no steady location for such a system—trying to understand, even in the interest of refusing, the fascist state is a losing game. One can perhaps only locate its effects and map out those interstices where systems of inequity and exploitation fail (generating, one hopes, entry points for difference). Often, this leads to a wearied affective state where one is overwhelmed with the ubiquity of inequity and the violence of an active legacy of exploitation. At the same time, being weary is entangled with casting a wary eye towards what might come next; bracing oneself for the ensuing example of the violent suppression of others. Weary/wary is an exhausting state where the sense of the present is overwhelmed by an unrelenting violent history that, in turn, offers a future of little promise or change. The force of the past repeating a future can instigate a type of exhaustive stasis; creative potential exchanged for the closure of what is possible.

To be weary/wary, then, is to become exhausted. As Rosi Braidotti (2020) similarly explains, the world can often seem too much and, "too-much-ness is one of the sources of exhaustion, which marks so much of our current predicament" (p. 4). The weary/wary predicament "ultimately brings about a shrinkage of our ability to take *in* and *on* the world that we are in, simply because it hurts too much to take in and on" (Braidotti 2020, p. 4; original emphases). When confronted with the necessary practice of recognition (a taking *in*, of sorts) in order to refuse (a practice of taking *on*) we perhaps shortchange our capacity to enact alternatives to the status quo. In this way, to become weary/wary is to risk cutting short or otherwise enclosing our potential—the world is too much and so we close off, exhausted.

Sara Ahmed (2019) emphasizes that such exhaustion can articulate as a governing institutional strategy: "Exhaustion can be a management technique: you tire people out so they are too tired to address what makes them too tired" (p. 162). In this instance, exhaustion is employed as a mechanism for maintaining the (exhausting) status quo—exhaustion as a strategic form of governance. This exhausted state has very material effects as those who bear the brunt of exploitation are more apt to endure long-term health problems (increased risk for diabetes, high blood pressure, anxiety, etc.); the body can only endure so much. And, it is the logic of late capitalism that insists such health disparities extend from individualized inadequacies, not collective trauma (that type-2 diabetes or hypertension, for example, are solely a result of poor eating habits or laziness; character defaults of the individual). Governing through exhaustion, then, marks inequity on the bodies of the exploited and individualizes the effects of such marking through assertions of moral failing (that there is something inherently delinquent in those who suffer the long-term consequences of exploitation).

The simultaneity of this exploitative collectivization and individuation is a marker of current instantiations of fascism. No longer a simple description of an authoritarian regime bent on increasing the geography of its rule, contemporary manifestations of fascism articulate as a type of autogenetic force that animates a particularly devastating way of being; an ontological isomorphism that refuses difference through the hungry repetition of dominant relations and identities. As Brian Massumi (2015) notes, present-day articulations of fascism extend as a type of ontopower, animated through a "fear-based collective individuation" (p, 187). The result is what Foucault (1983) deemed "the fascism in us all, in our heads and in our everyday behavior, the fascism that causes us to love power, to desire the very thing that dominates and exploits us" (p. xiii). As an exploitative way of being, fascism generates its own extension through manufacturing the very desire to continue the normalizing processes and practices through which it articulates. This is done through the fracturing of relational modes of being, a forced and violent embrace of the normalized and fully governed individual (the force of "collective individuation" that Massumi references above). As Braidotti (2019) notes, fascism articulates as "this totalitarian entity that dispels relational connections and instils suspicion and hatred. It leads to scapegoating instead of pursuing adequate understandings of our conditions" (p. 179). As such, fascism generates both a way of being and a means of interpreting our contemporary moment that fixates on individual triumphs of sameness through the violent excision of difference; fascism effects on onto-epistemological levels. The result is a generative force that overwhelms even the most careful of critics, producing a collective exhaustion that serves the dominant and exploitative status quo. Further, such exploitation is amplified by the collusion of fascism with processes of late capitalism in our contemporary moment. This strategic entanglement manufactures a type of consumptive exploitation that engages potential as a resource for its extension.

As Ahmed (2019) notes, there is an effective intimacy within capitalism between exploitation and exhaustion: "to exploit something or somebody you must exhaust their potential. A potential becomes that which must be exhausted" (p. 56). This is to situate exhaustion within a capitalistic relation that consumes resources to function—potential is the resource that capitalism comes to dominate, even exhaust. Of course, it is the very nature of an exploitative relation that the dominant "uses" the resources of some other for its subsistence and growth. Once a resource is exhausted, the system moves on.

Indeed, capitalism and fascism are conjoined through their entangled dependence on exploitative relations for their function. It is perhaps the burden of our contemporary moment that the two coincide in such devastating fashion—the fascist, white supremacist state engaging capitalism as a means to exhaust the potential of its citizenry. Once exhausted, one's ability to envision a difference becomes challenging at best and one remains within the closure of possibility; potential exhausted to possibility.

Simply stated, to consider the possible is to remain bound by the limiting determinations of conventional logic—possibility remains circumscribed by normalizing logic processes and favors repetition over experimentation. Thus, to think "what is possible" is to be governed by the limits imposed in the contemporary moment. Potential, on the other hand, remains open-ended and exceeds the logics of convention, pointing to a future yet unknown; ways of becoming that cannot be assumed or prescribed through convention. Potential is fully experimental—a challenge to what is through a creative exploration of becoming. Thus, exhaustion as a "management technique" effects a strategic shift away from potential (that which might yet become) and towards possibility (a future already defined by the logic of convention). *A potential truncated to the* possible.[1] In such circumstance one perhaps embraces the limitations of the possible in order to manage one's exploitative circumstance; a coping mechanism amidst the unrelenting forces of fascism and capitalism. The confines of limited change (even repetition) are thus embraced as a mechanism to *make do* amidst present circumstance; speculative imagination (what might yet become) exchanged for practiced resignation (what inevitably will be).

Further, the governed reorientation from potential to possibility also trends a shift from collective imagination to individualized apathy and isolated resignation. That is, the open-ended nature of potential generates the promise of new relation, alternative connection not yet determined by the status quo. Thus, potential can never be isolated or bound within some individual subject (potential does not operate within closed systems or truncated processes). Instead, potential requires an imaginative experimentation with the present in order to create an untold future. Possibility, on the other hand, requires no such experimentation, bound as it is to contemporary formations of being. As such, possibility operates quite well within individualized and isolated environs, requiring none of the imaginative engagement of potential. Whereas potential promotes a creative experimentation with perceived limits (what can an entity do, what might it yet become?), possibility reinscribes the bounds of already-experienced reality (what remains within the bounds of the possible?). More than simply definitional differentiation, engaging potential or possibility has very material effects. Whereas the former offers new creations and challenges to the status quo, the latter posits a need for refining what is already known or experienced. And, refinement can only go so far—it often runs its course, calling forth an apathetic affect—how will anything change if we perpetually dwell within the confines of the possible? In this way, the emphasis of the possible over potential is strategic, binding one to concerns for reform over and above an enlivening engagement with revolution. To engage potential, then, is to refuse the governing processes and limits that circumscribe our contemporary moment in order to confect anew—a challenge to what is in order to create new conditions for what might yet become. Inquiry work has a role in this, I think, as it entails mapping the limits of the possible in order to activate a transgressive alternative; what might we yet become? To do so, we must similarly transgress the limitations of our exhaustion, fracturing the determined connection between exhaustion and governance.

Becoming Exhausted

Perhaps exhaustion extends from a forever-debilitating practice of trying to "keep up" with (or coming to grips with) governing processes that persistently modulate, altering formation in order to continue exploitative control. As Deleuze (1992) notes, this modulation is a characteristic of "control societies" and articulates "like a self-deforming cast that will continuously change from one moment to the other" (p. 4). Control societies govern through management, a protean capacity to shape-shift even as they enforce an ever-changing array of normalizing molds to which individuals must acquiesce. The result is continual exhaustion as one must repeatedly relearn seemingly new ways of being governed. Like being out of breath through running on an unbalanced treadmill—exhausted by the effort to achieve stasis—simply "keeping up" loses its orienting function and one perhaps releases to newly controlled shapes achieved through a changing series of "self-deforming" casts. For Deleuze, such circumstances extend control as the management of an endless array of activities that generate new (de)formations and corresponding practices: "in the societies of control one is never finished with anything" (p. 5). The modulated/modulating controlled subject is a life-long learning participant, forever engaged in an endless array of controlling tasks, processes and participations. This is a repetitious feedback loop that conjoins the exploited subject with the undulating modulations of governing processes. In such circumstance, normalizing institutions articulate as "metastable states coexisting in one and the same modulation, like a universal system of deformation" (p. 5). Control societies are exhausting indeed, requiring as they do for individuals to reinvent their own exploitative formation in order to achieve some semblance of recognition.

And yet, despite this exhaustion, despite our shared weary/wary state, we endure. The exchange of potential for possibility is never complete; there is always more. And, this enduring process binds us relationally as one never endures alone or in isolation. As Rosi Braidotti (2011) notes, the process of enduring is inherently relational and open-ended, absent the conventional trappings of closure that extend from normalized assumptions of the cartesian subject: "The capacity to endure is collective; it is to be shared…. It is a moment in a process of becoming" (p. 164). Endurance, then, is a resistive and relational process.

Importantly, enduring together counters the exploitative forces of collective individuation that drive both capitalism and fascism. Further, to endure necessitates a fracturing of the seemingly total and complete Cartesian subject, the learned and repeated object of exploitative systems. Because they are always singular, Cartesian subjects do not endure: they conclude. This stems from the notion that the Cartesian (or humanist) subject is, by definition, closed and, to a degree, fixed. Thus, when the subject ends (a death imposed) it is no more. There thus remains only the potential for the subject to become something else—no longer a closed subject but a differently conceived entity that is not contained/containable. In this sense, the subject dissipates towards a differently relational becoming. With this dissolution extends the disruption of the numerous assumptions and rationales that made the subject possible in the first place.

In many ways, to endure is to return to the promise of potential; the radical claim that one might yet become otherwise. This enduring potential draws forth the ethically-laden work of manifesting the conditions necessary for enduring. And, it is here that one perhaps locates a productive role for inquiry: through inquiry one might disrupt the closed repetitions of convention and confect the conditions necessary to endure differently, becoming anew. Inquiry works towards a more than adequate understanding of our contemporary moment.

For Braidotti (2011), ethical work includes creating the conditions necessary for endurance. In part, this includes a relational bond that continues despite (or, in many ways, because of) a desire for transformation, for becoming otherwise. This transformative potential generatively works towards sustainability—we endure together and through such acts create a sustainable network for change. Thus, it is that to engage in inquiry is to, in many ways, embrace a politics of affirmation, one that animates Braidotti's own belief in the transformative potential imbued within relational endurance. Further, the work of inquiry becomes an ethically-infused claim that we might create the conditions for becoming anew, breaking the repetitious patterns of exploitation that maintain the status quo and govern an assumed shift from potential to possibility. This is to manufacture potential out of the very weary/wary state that extends from living in our world and in our times.

For Braidotti (2011, 2019), endurance is both temporal (dealing with duration, or lasting in time) and spatial (having to do with the body, the "enfleshment" of affect). As Braidotti writes, endurance,

> entails temporal duration, thus proposing the notions of the subject as an entity that survives and lasts. It also refers to spatial elements, the ability to withstand and sustain changes and transformation and to enact them affirmatively in environmental, social and affective terms. Endurance involves affectivity and joy, but it also means putting up with hardship and physical pain.
>
> *(2019, p. 172)*

Enduring survival is hard work and my aim here is not to romanticize the resistive process of continuing on in violently exploitative circumstance. Indeed, as Braidotti notes, enduring is more than an abstract idea—it marks bodies through "hardship and physical pain." At the same time, it remains important to note that the relationally-creative process of enduring is also marked by potential, an affirmative affect of transformation—through enduring one might yet become anew. This transformative potential is imbued in all elements of lasting survival and those who engage in inquiry are perhaps charged with an ethical responsibility to confect the relations and conditions necessary to endure differently, to generate eventful becomings that are sustainable in process and practice. To do so, it seems, one must recognize the productive ambiguity and challenge that extends from being weary/wary. In some ways, this is to learn from the very state of exhaustion that we perhaps initially seek to avoid or otherwise manage into the limitations of possibility.

As Deleuze (1995) notes, there exists a degree of active ambiguity among the exhausted: "you are not passive: you press on, but toward nothing. You were tired by something, but exhausted by nothing" (p. 4). At first glance, to be exhausted might entail being overwhelmed by indeterminacy: one looks for the origins of exhaustion and finds nothing; one seeks to locate an end and senses no conclusion. Yet, despite this, one presses on—one endures—and herein lies a potential amidst ambiguity. This pressing on is perhaps an example of enduring, continuing despite exhaustive-exhausting circumstance. As Deleuze asserts, there is a decided lack of specificity to becoming exhausted—one can never point to the origin of exhaustion, the cause of this exhausted effect. Nor can one locate a space where this ontological state will end—what must happen for one to no longer become exhausted? Thus, to become weary/wary is to exist outside both causal and prescriptive logic: there is no cause to the exhausted effect; no prescribed end or destination that concludes the exhausted sate. *One is weary without origin; wary without end.* And, yet again, "you press on;" you endure.

Indeed, Deleuze (1995) goes on to locate potential within the exhausted as it is through exhaustion that the limitations of possibility are realized and transformed: "only the exhausted can exhaust the possible" (p. 5). This sense of concluding the possible extends from a seemingly contradictory doubleness imbued within the exhausted that includes a productive distancing from normalizing value and logic systems and, at the same time, a close attention to the details of the present. As Deleuze writes, one is simultaneously "sufficiently disinterested" and "sufficiently scrupulous" to "abolish the real" (p. 5). To be both formless and specific is the promise of the exhausted. Given our contemporary moment, this doubled state refuses the preformed logics and locations that extend from fascist processes (a "disinterested" relation to "the real") and specifically engages practices animated by an alternative potential (a "scrupulous" engagement in what might yet become). It is the exhausted that might "abolish the real"—not just refusing but transforming the ontological realities of living in our shared present. And, it is in this enduring doubleness (a refusal of possibility entangled with a detailed recognition of a potential difference) that inquiry might find its footing. Given the violent tragedy of our times, the work of inquiry to "abolish the real" takes on ethical urgency: we need to set the stage for enactments of a different potential. Indeed, though it seems within this contemporary moment that to engage in inquiry is an exhaustive endeavor we necessarily "press on, but toward nothing;" the ethical work of confecting anew in a fascist world order.

Specifically, Deleuze (1995) articulates the exhausted as a type of "amnesic witness" who remains "on the lookout for words, for voices, for sounds" (p. 6). The exhausted refuses the logics of the past and witnesses a present unfolding that might be sensed anew, without the enforced definitional determinisms that extend from the repetition of a fascist state. There is thus potential in the simultaneity of resistive forgetting and precise witnessing: an exhausted lookout as a resistive witness; becoming weary/wary towards indeterminate potential. Returning to Ahmed (2019) for a moment, we are reminded that "exhaustion and rebellion can come from the same place" (p. 228). There is always more work to be done.

Given the potential identified by both Deleuze and Ahmed in transformation and rebellion out of exhaustion, it is perhaps helpful to recap the claims made thus far and relate them to processes of inquiry, which I understand as means for confecting anew. First, becoming weary/wary involves disconnecting forced processes of recognition and repetition (those extending from the trying activities of taking in and on) in order to effect a potential difference. Second, such a position marks a relational capacity that extends from our collective endurance; we continue on, but towards an ambiguous future. Third, an enduring exhaustion extends a transformative potential that remains animated by the force of our weary/wary and exhausted state. And, fourth, it is in this spatio-temporal entanglement that inquiry might work to confect anew a potential and future otherwise. With such claims in mind, we might locate the ethical work of inquiry as the creation of conditions for transforming exhaustion from repetitive governance towards a relational difference. Inquiry thus enacted as a resistive practice of abolishing the real in favor of generating new potential; to inquire such that we might become differently. This, of course, is philosophical and material work and perhaps extends from the practice of standing vigil that so intrigues Foucault.

Foucault's Vigil

Foucault's (2015) essay, "Standing Vigil for the Day to Come," reviews a work of fiction by Roger Laporte (the novel *La Veille*) and, in doing so, provides a useful perspective on a relational in-between, what contemporary theorists perhaps understand as a process of "becoming" that (among other things) holds an implicit critique of the Cartesian closed subject. In this essay, Foucault offers the practice of "standing vigil" as an emplaced and embodied positioning on the transgressive cusp of change. One stands vigil in/on the threshold, orienting towards what might come and recognizing the inevitable change to what already was.

As I have noted elsewhere (Kuntz, 2020b), the threshold marks an entangled relation of limits and transgressions. Limits always contain their potential dissolution, their capacity to transgress. Thus, though seemingly fixed, limits are always open to becoming something else. Consequently, "limits and transgressions are insatiably incomplete, always partial" (Kuntz, 2020b, p. 6). It is in their indeterminacy that limits and transgressions are of use to projects of transformation. As a means to enact such change, one works to *map*, *contest* and *refuse* conventional limits in order to generate a relational difference. In this way, one uses the very stuff of a limit to generate transgression—to transform possibility into potential: "Thus it is not enough to simply strive to break a limit: one must use the material of the limit to generate something else. This is a creative or experimental relation to limits, one that manufactures difference where once was only repetition" (p. 6). This is perhaps the work of inquiry as a means to generate the conditions necessary for transformation—engaging the "material of the limit" to confect anew. This transformative practice is animated by an ethical force, the determination that "our current circumstances are untenable—we need a different future" (p. 7). Thus, it is that productive change comes from working the limits—mapping, contesting and refusing the confines of what is in favor of the more indeterminate and potentially transformative space of what might yet become.

For Foucault (2015) keeping vigil extends a similarly indeterminate time and space as seen in the "transgressively new." Temporally, a vigil occurs "not after evening but before morning, without any other 'before'" (p. 218). The vigil exists in an undetermined present, not bound by the force of the past and not yet claimed by the possible future. Foucault thus situates a vigil as forever ensconced in the "eve:" "this day which has not yet come, which will perhaps never come. What says "not yet" to the next day stands vigil: the eve is *the day which precedes*. Or more accurately, it's that which precedes each day" (p. 218; original emphasis). The eve presents a productive pause to the momentum of determination, an interstice in the overwhelming extension of late capitalism. To dwell within the eve is to begin a forceful refusal, saying "not yet" to the otherwise inevitable claims of convention. Thus, it is that standing vigil situates one on the precipice, a transgressive threshold of becoming anew that articulates as a practice of resistance. This is an imminent positioning, one that refuses the closure of things coming to pass: "it is today, even now, this simultaneous shortfall and excess that delimits and surpasses the day" (p. 218).

Through orienting within the eve, standing vigil blurs the otherwise-defining claim of complete subjectivity: "it is not me who is on watch in the eve's vigilance; it's the recoil of the coming day" (Foucault 2015, p. 218). The vigil merges one with the retreat of what has yet-to-be; processes of becoming deindividualize what once was in favor of a productive, undifferentiated potential. Through standing vigil one practices transgressive contradiction: "wide eyes that admit yet ward off the night" (p. 219). This practice articulates as a type of "attentive endurance" that allows in (what has yet to come) and keeps out (what has just become). Weary/wary indeed.

Importantly, for Foucault (2015) standing vigil takes place within an open and equally indeterminate space: "the lookout is made in the open countryside" and "does not take refuge in any fortress" (p. 220). The openness of the countryside dissolves any distinct subjecthood and in that dissolution, more is seen: "In a sense, everything is visible because there is no point of view, no lost profile, no perspective that settles in the distance; but nothing, in fact, is visible since what is near is also quite far away in this careful and attentive elimination of any accommodation" (p. 220). The vigil necessarily removes these orienting markers that would otherwise bring about limiting definition, absenting claims on what things are based on the specificity of their relation. Instead, the vigil refuses the concrete positioning that manifests an individualized way of being or point of view—the near and far of perspective that is so important to claims on subjecthood. When such distinguishing markers dissipate, "everything is visible" (potential becomes through blurred undifferentiation) and, consequently "nothing, in fact, is visible" (the known or possible loses the dominance of meaning, or meaning-made).

For Foucault (2015) transgressive space-time disrupts conventional epistemological practices through its very immanent placement. This might be seen as the location of philosophical inquiry, articulating as,

> almost unthinkable since thinking and speaking are only possible following it. It itself cannot be thought, recognized, or expressed until the day has arrived and night returned to its uncertainty. Such that we can no longer think but this provision—rock of our stupidity: we do *not yet* think."
>
> *(219; original emphasis)*

Such it is that philosophical work is not thinking (or, *not yet* thinking). Thinking can only occur after the vigil has ended; after the transgressive moment has dissipated into certainty (night into day). Thus, it is (to return to the title of this chapter) that "confecting anew" requires more than thinking—it is through philosophical inquiry that thinking blurs into conceptual creation and a different ontological becoming.

The vigil extends as a place where philosophical inquiry might occur—the precipice of the *not yet* calls forth a potential transformation within the space and time of the vigil. Foucault (2015) thus shifts to considerations of

> where thought heads indefinitely towards non-thought, which glistens before it, and silently sustains the possibility of thought. Unthought which is not an obscure object to know but rather the opening of thought itself... it never ceases expecting itself, remaining on the lookout in the advance on its own day."
>
> *(p. 222)*

This process shifts the aim of such work: to think not "the true" but "the just" (p. 222). The vigil, then, extends an ethical orientation: to think "the just" is to assert a claim on what might yet become; an ethical practice of difference making. It is here that the act of standing vigil takes on the potential of virtue—on the lookout for what might yet become in order to generate the just.

From Vigil to Vigilance

Of course, standing vigil can often blur into a practice of maintaining the contemporary status quo, looking out for threats to the normative order that one feels charged to govern into docility. Here, the practice of "looking out" coincides with a sense of necessary preparation and preemption: threats to the status quo are assumed always out there, forever on the horizon, and thus one must actively work to challenge and usurp such revolutionary potential. Such it is that the promise of the vigil is reduced to the practice of maintenance and the potential for becoming otherwise is exchanged for the active challenge of replicating what already is. In such circumstance, standing vigil transforms into exercises of vigilance. The preemptive nature of such vigilant practices reveals them as driven by the force of ontopower, a constitutive relation that coincides in particularly troubling ways with the context of late capitalism and its legacy of exploitative relations. Vigilant preemption requires an imaginative capacity to assume a future threat and a governing determination to intervene in the conditions and relations that might coincide to affect such a challenge to the contemporary status quo. In this way, preemption "operates in the element of vagueness and objective uncertainty" (Massumi, 2015, p. 15). On the threshold, preemption creates a threat in order to make possible acts of governing intervention. As such, preemption is endlessly proliferative and disturbingly imaginative—shape-shifting amidst ambiguity in order to produce a future previously undetermined even as it claims that future as a threat to what is.

Indeed, the collusion of late capitalism with contemporary formations of fascism is, in many ways, driven by the force of preemption. Late capitalism seeks to extend consumptive processes into the very ontological formations that contribute to our sense of being. Similarly, fascism operates on principles of collective individuation (Masumi, 2015)—that one becomes an individual subject through subscribing to the normalizing processes, practices and ontological assumptions of the collective. Vigilance extends from the consuming determination to maintain the exploitative present through a series of preemptive acts—conjuring events that have yet to occur in order to reinscribe the status quo. This element of preemption, then, seeks to consume and exhaust any potential to become otherwise. Perhaps there exists a role for philosophical inquiry to short-circuit the forceful intersection of late capitalism and fascism through activating limits to generate transgressive alternatives to our contemporary moment. Inquiry enacted as a means to stand vigil in exhausting times, conspiring towards different creations; inquiry as a practice of confecting anew.

Philosophical Inquiry as an Ethical Practice of Confecting Anew

I have elsewhere termed philosophical inquiry as a series of ethically-oriented practices that "simultaneously critique the contemporary moment and manifest an open-ended and yet to be known potential; the not-yet that is a radical challenge to what has come to be" (Kuntz, 2020a, p. 45). Given its engagement with the present and determination to open a future unknown, philosophical inquiry might be understood as an enacted vigil, dwelling within and making use of indeterminacy. Philosophical inquiry might also extend from our weary/wary state—the resolute pressing on that is a marker of exhausted endurance. And so, I find value in philosophical inquiry as a generative means to work through and with our contemporary moment (challenging though that may be).

An important element of philosophical inquiry extends from its determination to map the present in order to locate spaces of difference through which transformation might occur. This is, to use Foucauldian terminology, generating a "history of the present." Importantly, this mapping emphasizes questions of how the contemporary moment operates, not why (there is, of course, no search for an essential cause or origin that produced these current effects and relations). Diagramming the present affords one a consideration of its limits—those spaces where convention demands closure and a reinvigorated repetition of normalized ways of being and knowing. Here, philosophical inquiry is animated by a belief that we might become otherwise as the limit-as-enclosure is reengaged as transgressive potential.

This belief in a potential otherwise is conjoined with an ethical claim that present exploitative relations are untenable and unjust. Thus, we must become otherwise and do so through an ongoing engagement with the very material of assumed limits. In this way, philosophical inquiry eschews the simplistic (and oddly romanticized) vision of philosophical work taking place at a comfortable distance from the material world. Instead, philosophical inquiry remains fully ensconced in the material moment even as it articulates as practices of virtuous refusal. Out of this refusal extends an equally ethically-laden practice of confecting anew—orienting towards a potential that has yet to be fully realized or known.

Thus, it is that philosophical inquiry necessarily entails acts of difficult recognition (we are bound by and responsible for these tragic circumstances), belief (we might be otherwise) and virtue (we must become differently). And, it must be noted, this entangled relation of recognition, belief and virtue situates philosophical inquiry as a materialist methodology—generated within and through the very material conditions and relations through which we live our lives. As such, philosophical inquiry works to generate the conditions necessary for ontological transformation. It does so through a materialist practice of standing vigil, confecting anew amidst an indeterminate transgressive space of becoming. Philosophical inquiry is, in short, an ethically-laden making; a means of generating "the just" in circumstances that overwhelm through perpetuating injustice. To engage in such work is to become exhausted—to use the very stuff of being weary/wary such that we have no choice but to endure towards a difference. Animated by the force of virtue, philosophical inquiry locates the limits of our contemporary moment such that newly transgressive confections might activate a different potential.

Conclusion

Somewhat in closing, I return to a question first offered in the introduction: "what does it mean to inquire, in this moment, when the world seems perpetually afire?" Responding to this question from a weary/wary state, I orient through an enacted vigil, registering the exploitative limits of the present and casting a critical eye towards transformative potential; a type of exhausted endurance for enacted change. In many ways, I remain emboldened through Braidotti's (2019) notion that we might practice a "pragmatic engagement with the present…in order to collectively construct conditions that transform and empower our capacity to act ethically and produce social horizons of hope, or sustainable futures" (p. 173). For me, inquiry is part-and-parcel of such resistive and productive practice. Through inquiry we engage with the present as a Deleuzian "amnesic witness," blurring the governing processes and practices of fascism such that they lose their precise purpose; creating relational conditions through which specific forms of resistive potential become anew. Through inquiry we might engage the present to break its violent hold on our very being; utilizing the circumstances that enforce our exhaustion such that we might become otherwise. Through inquiry we stand vigil, lookouts for potential change, refusing the governing limitations of the status quo and using the material of our contemporary moment to generate a transformative difference—confecting anew in a fascist world.

Note

1 For a more thorough treatment of the possible and a potential see Kuntz, 2019.

References

Ahmed, S. (2019). *What's the Use?* Durham: Duke University Press.
Braidotti, R. (2011). *Nomadic Theory: The Portable Rosi Braidotti*. New York: Columbia University Press.
Braidotti, R. (2019). *Posthuman Knowledge*. Cambridge: Polity Press.
Braidotti, R. (2020). 'We' Are In This Together, But We Are Not One and the Same. *Bioethical Inquiry*. Retrieved from https://doi.org/10.1007/s11673-020-10017-8
Deleuze, G. (1992). Postscript on the societies of control. *October*, 59, 3–7.
Deleuze, G. (1995). The exhausted. *Substance*, *24*(3), 3–28.
Deleuze, G., & Parnet, C. (1996). *Dialogues*. Paris: Flammarion.
Foucault, M. (1983). Preface. In G. Deleuze, & F. Guattari (Eds.) (Hurley, Seem, & Lane, trans). *Anti-Oedipus: Capitalism and Schizophrenia* (pp. xi–xix). Minneapolis: University of Minnesota Press.
Foucault, M. (2015). Standing vigil for the day to come. *Foucault Studies*, *19*, 217–223.
Kuntz, A. M. (2019). *Qualitative Inquiry, Cartography, and the Promise of Material Change*. London: Routledge Press.
Kuntz, A. M. (2020a). Foucauldian practices: Philosophical inquiry as virtuous enactments for material change. *ACCESS: Contemporary Issues in Education*, *40*(1), 41–46. Retrieved from https://doi.org/10.46786/ac20.8961
Kuntz, A. M. (2020b). "Piercing this wall": Truth-making in a fascist world. *Qualitative Inquiry*. doi.org/10.1177/1077800420934153.
Massumi, B. (2015). *Ontopower: War, Powers, and the State of Perception*. Durham, NC: Duke University Press. Retrieved from https://doi.org/10.1215/9780822375197

SECTION II

Performative Futures

3

BETWEENERS: OUR COMMON HUMANITY IN REPRESSIVE TIMES

Claudio Moreira and Marcelo Diversi

For those experiencing systemic violence, the human experience must have always felt lived in repressive times. For those experiencing systemic exclusion, life must have always felt maddeningly unfair. For those experiencing erasure, present and past, life must have felt like an unresolvable dissonance between the materiality of body and the mirror devoid of reflection. Human experience must have always moved back and forth between collective tribal experiences of Us versus Them, between the immense nuances of human kinds, as in the temporary and quickly moving identities we experience according to the temporary and quickly moving contexts of everyday life (Berreby, 2008).

> How can we find each other's humanity?
> We are writing on election day when only one of us is able to cast a vote
> We are writing with hope and from the heart (Pelias, 2004)
> Hope to change the world.

Democrats versus Republicans, men versus women, cisgender versus transgender, white versus colored, meat eaters versus vegans, locals versus foreigners, rural versus urban and so many other prosaic tribal tropes are ultimately oversimplifications of complex border-crossing identities that are as inevitable in the origins of our species as they are avoidable by the keen human ability to find common ground under circumstances that highlight our shared humanity. The COVID-19 pandemic, to hone in on the present day, has dramatically highlighted our shared human vulnerability and global connections, with endless documented instances of opposing tribes suddenly coming together for the sake of survival and organized front against this new strain of a coronavirus, itself another border-crossing species. The borders—all borders—are always more permeable than a casual glance can understand. And we cross these borders more often, and with more grace, than most people notice.

At the beginning of the pandemic, for instance, the Chinese government delivered boxes of much needed medical supplies to Italy, the first Western country to declare a total lockdown as the pandemic raged out of control and threatened to overwhelm its public health system (Gambardella, 2020). It would have been an unlikely gesture in the pre-pandemic tense politics of East versus West. The label-message on each box of medical supplies, chosen by the Chinese government, made the central point of our own text here in a lovely, powerful poetic way. The labels carried a rough translation of words from a Roman philosopher, Seneca, that said "We are waves of the same sea, leaves of the same tree, flowers of the same garden" (Gambardella, 2020). To be sure, we are not equally prepared for nor equally privileged in facing this pandemic. We certainly are not on the same proverbial boat, even though we are all trying to survive the same giant storm. Yet, our inherent common humanity is being underscored by a virus that does not discriminate between Democrats and Republicans, Christians and Muslims, tribes of all colors and political identity shades.

The West tends to Orientalize the East when searching for platitudes declaring ancient wisdom (Said, 1978). China turned this cliché on its head and used one of Italy's own ancient philosophers as it made an offering of solidarity and human unity. Gestures like this shed a bright light on our ability and potential to cherish our common humanity while acknowledging our cultural and tribal inclinations and differences. To the best of our anthropological knowledge, human history has always been marked by tribalism: Us versus Them, my kind over yours and often viciously so when life gets tough. Yet it has also been marked by cooperation, collaboration, kindness, generosity, openness between tribes, between sides, between standpoints, between a drive to care for self above everyone else and the ability to care for BOTH self AND others.

> We, again, find ourselves at a crossroad!
> Humanity over corporate greed.
> Lives over money
> Racial democracy over structural racism
> Xenophobia, homophobia
> Both under the thump of divisive patriarchal and neoliberal systems
> We see the wounds
> Caused by the USA president's performance of

White supremacy,
Toxic masculinity
Embedded in hegemonic discourses of hate and violence against
The Other
The other Other
Breathe deeply
Try to stay calm
We have to stay calm
We have to stay as clear-headed as we can
To resist the accelerating march of authoritarianism
To connect, to cooperate, to coordinate, to join forces
With all brothers and sisters, and everyone in between, who
Want to imagine and create a more inclusive
Kinder
World

We, again, find ourselves deep in this ontological, epistemological, and ethical space of struggling to muster energy to care for BOTH our tribe AND our common humanity across all political divides. We struggle to understand how so many fellow citizens voted for a president and political party that have made exclusion, division, denial of science and scholarship the compass of their political praxis between 2017 and 2020, global pandemic and all. Our individual citizen sides are disgusted with the realization that almost half of all voters of the 2020 general election in the United States can still find ways to support a president that lies about both mundane and very consequential things, and everything in between, a president who chooses to claim in broad daylight that the pandemic is "rounding the corner and going away" in the very month the country is tabulating record numbers of new daily infections. Beyond the pandemic, the dishonesty is hard to fathom and will certainly have enduring consequences for the United States and beyond (Baker, 2020). We struggle to understand how almost half of all voters in the 2020 general election in the United States can still rationalize ways to support such vile incompetence carried out in plain sight, with publicly displayed pride even, with the goals of fostering national division, distrust in journalism, science, knowledge and the very government that he has been in charge of for the last four years, and for which he is willing to cheat to win again, at the cost of democracy, U.S. history, and everyone and anyone else who is not blindly loyal and submissive. He claimed victory at the end of Election Day before many states and millions of legal votes had been counted. We come from a country in South America that has been called a banana republic, here and there, in the last hundred years. Such an illegal victory claim would have no legs even in that country, at least not without a more crafted plot for context. Yet there is absolutely no judicial consequence for his illegal claim. This president claims to be for "law and order," yet he is breaking the law by claiming victory before all legal votes are counted. He is trying to stop the vote count via Twitter, mob incitement and frivolous lawsuits.

It is disorienting. Where are we? Where are the legendary checks and balances? How can an intellectually limited pathological narcissist unravel the oldest and longest lasting democracy, however imperfect, in such a short time? He is an unfortunate example of the immense power of narratives and storytelling.

> We both came to life under dictatorship in Brazil
> No right to vote
> Senate and congress were closed
> Generals were the "presidents"
> And yes, we emigrated to the U.S. on our own volition
> Here, we are accented tongues in the "land of freedom"
> We experience life together
> Through thick and thin
> And suffer together with the stories of this president's cruelty
> 545 children separated from their parents at the southern border
> Now many of these children and parents can't find each other
> They cannot Be Reunited
> How come?
> How come 45% of us in this country cannot imagine these children as
>   their own?
> Two days after the 2020 election, at least 70 million Americans
> Voted to support such cruel policies
> A bit too much for a country that likes to call itself the "leader of the free
>   world"
> We must breathe deeply

★★★

Our intellectual sides, at the same time and in conflicting and messy ways, are simply observing the American experiment in one of its most chaotic times in history, helplessly waiting to see whether we can, somehow, collectively, hold this imperfect yet promising democracy together when the sitting president repeatedly refuses to say on national television that he would concede if his opponent won the 2020 presidential election. On November 3rd and 5th of 2020, we watched the sitting president of the United States go on national television and claim victory before millions of legal votes were counted all over the country, while also making false and unsubstantiated allegations of voting fraud. With impunity. Where are the checks and balances now that we really need them?

Intellectually, we understand that the central narrative of exclusion of the Other, a narrative centered on hatred, tribalism, fear-mongering, clearly connects the dots between our past and the present, between colonization and state-sanctioned voting suppression, between our history as told by male European settlers and the need to support the Black Lives Matter movement in 2020. About half of voting citizens in the United States, in 2020, are no more, or less, than modern-time pioneers vying to conquer this land, with no regrets or qualms about pursuing this present-day conquest by following the strategies used by earlier European settlers: step and kneel on the necks of women, people of color, indigenous peoples, gender non-conforming folks and even their poorer White brethren.

> Rapists, drug lords, criminal aliens
> We have been called
> By the Man in Power
> Yes, that House is extremely White
> Talking about that House, the White House, a wall has been built overnight, in the election night, to keep protestors out. It is a wall to protect the 250 plus White Rich People invited to celebrate the election's results with the White Man in Power! Yes, He built a wall after all. It cannot be just us who see the irony, right? White man, White House, White wall...
> White, White, White, White, White, White, White, White, White, White, White, White
> "One thing we've seen in a lot of the Black community, which is mostly Democrat, is that President (Donald) Trump's policies are the policies that can help people break out of the problems that they're complaining about...But he can't want them to be successful more than they want to be successful," said the Son in Law, the trust fund baby.
> We struggle...

We struggle in the ontological, epistemological and pedagogical spaces between unleashing our fury against the "wrong side," against those we deem to be the oppressors, and the intellectual realization that *the only way out of this polarization* is to imagine, create and cultivate, against all odds, paths of unity, reconciliation, healing together, dreaming together of a kinder social-political-economical system that channels our energy away from Us versus Them tribalism to Us and Them cooperation and problem-solving. We don't have easy or hard fixes for this reframing. But we know that we can dedicate our best efforts to our teaching, scholarship and praxis (Diversi & Moreira, 2009, 2018). We need inspiration and mighty support for that. So we seek inspiration in and from those who came before us and on whose broad shoulders we stand:

> You write in order to change the world, knowing perfectly well that you probably can't, but also knowing that literature is indispensable to the world… The world changes according to the way people see it, and if you alter, even but a millimeter the way people look at reality, then you can change it.
>
> *(Baldwin, 1979, p. 3)*

We find ourselves returning to Paulo Freire whenever confronted with essentialist approaches of Us versus Them. We believe in education in all aspects, in all levels, inside and outside formal schooling. Freire has taught us to read the world—more than that, he taught us that conscientization has a direct relation to systems of oppression. How are we? Where do we come from? Whose lives are valued at the expense of others? How do demonizing narratives of oppressed groups become so powerful? How were dehumanizing narratives about immigration essential for a fascist-leaning regime to gain elections in the USA? How is it possible that a QAnon believer just got elected to the U.S. Congress to represent Georgia's 14th Congressional District? QAnon is NOT a conspiracy theory that aims at uniting us toward a more perfect union (LaFrance, 2020).

For us, all of these answers are about education, or the lack of a critical one. Education that wants to promote humanization rejects teaching that seeks to "deposit" information and embraces teaching that seeks to move students and teachers and everybody involved in this process, into praxis (i.e., action based on reflection of people upon their world with the conscious goal of transforming it), the foundation of true dialogue, the basis to find hope, the foundation of pacifist revolutions! Education gives us a sophisticated way to call conspiracy theories and neofascism bullshit, bullshit. And we can teach thousands of college students throughout our careers. We teach to name the elephant in the room: White supremacy, systemic racism, White fragility, politics of exclusion. We teach to denounce and challenge oppressive governments that promote racist public and private policies. We teach to expose the ideological cruelty the wealthy use to try and explain the thousands of children going to bed hungry every night in the most powerful country in the planet. Critical education gives us, all of us, the ability to teach, learn and strive for hope! As Freire (1995) wrote

> … while I certainly cannot ignore hopelessness as a concrete entity, nor turn a blind eye to the historical, economic, and social reasons that explain that hopelessness, I do not understand human existence, and the struggle needed to improve it, apart from hope and dream. Hope is an ontological need. Hopelessness is but hope that has lost its bearings, and become a distortion of that ontological need.
>
> *(p. 8)*

November 8, 2016

We remember this night four years ago
Claudio explaining the inexplicable to his then 14- and 12-year old children
Francisco asking at 2 a.m. if we would be able to stay in the country
Asking a few weeks later if he was a DACA child
A "dreamer"
No, Francisco, you were born here, both of you.
Analua, with tears in her eyes, "How can I exist as a young Latina in this
   country?"
Yes, we remember
Remember these 4 years of hatred, violence, genocide inside and abroad
By a politics of exclusion shaped and informed by ideologies of domination
The president is but a stand-in for the so called
Conservative mob
Breathe deeply
Stay clear-headed
To find our decolonizing ways out
To find each other's humanity
To encourage and to be inspired by the younger generation's idealism about
   inclusion and the possibility of change
Analua, now 18, already cast her vote!
"I vote for my whole family, the four of us."
We are writing right now without knowing what this election night will
   bring...
And it is difficult to dream...do we dare to...dream?
Yet we hope
And also, we hope that we will find the strength to keep fighting if this night
   brings us more 4 years of this nightmare, a nightmare that, unfortunately,
   is not a bad dream but a political reality, whose cruelty have killed many
   in the U.S. and abroad.

And we return to our question, how can we find each other's humanity?
And we return to the central embodied metaphor guiding our work together.
We are betweener bodies experiencing the world from the spaces in between
over-simplified identities, living between blurred borders, both cultural and
physical. We are border smugglers inhabiting the spaces in between dirty streets
and beautiful universities, committed to narrating visceral stories of blood and
profanities that bounce around among the excluded and oppressed, while also
hoping to help improve our understanding of the greater communality in our
human differences, to help all of us to understand our own different in-between
positionalities. Trying to create betweener autoethnographies from the places
we live and labor, the borders we keep crossing in our daily lives. We hope that

our work may create the possibility to be dangerous to power (Madison, 2010), to imagine a better world, to live meaningful lives, to keep hope alive. We have previously written that

> [s]ince joining each other in scholarship and profession, we have been bound by a commitment to ground the political back on the body, on the actual backs that reflect back the politics of exclusion of our times. We want our autoethnography to work as a magnifying glass on this reflection, the reflection that each body sends back to the relational world we live in. We want our autoethnography to examine, deconstruct, and trouble the reflection that each of our own bodies sends back to the intersections of race, gender, sexuality, nationality, and class shaping and informing our encounters with students, scholarly texts, and the politics of knowledge production.
>
> (*Diversi & Moreira, 2018, p. 110*)

We dare to imagine and fight for a better world, through our teaching, scholarship and everyday lives. Even though Trump has been defeated in the 2020 election, we have been around poverty and violence long enough that we know we don't elect saviors! It is in the grind of our daily routines, in our writings and research, in our activism inside and outside the classroom, that our concrete hope resides, that we find one of the possibilities to a path to expand the circle of us…to imagine a world of brothers and sisters and everybody in between, where discourses of hate cannot find a home, because this planet must be the home of all of us…

> In between countries and geographies
> In between HELL and NARRATIVE
> In between despair and hope
> We keep working because
> As our muse says
> We resist because we must
> There are no other options!

References

Baker, P. (2020, November 1). Dishonesty Has Defined the Trump Presidency. The Consequences Could Be Lasting. New York Times. Retrieved from https://www.nytimes.com/2020/11/01/us/politics/trump-presidency-dishonesty.html

Baldwin, J. (1979). Interview by Mel Atkins. *New York Times Book Review*, September 23, 3.

Berreby, D. (2008). *Us versus Them: The science of identity*. Chicago, IL: The University of Chicago Press.

Diversi, M., & Moreira, C. (2009). *Betweener Talk: Decolonizing Knowledge Production, Pedagogy, and Praxis*. Walnut Creek, CA: Left Coast Press.

Diversi, M., & Moreira, C. (2018). *Betweener Autoethnographies: A Path towards Social Justice.* New York: Routledge.

Freire, P. (1995). *Pedagogy of Hope: Reliving Pedagogy of the Oppressed* (R. R. Barr, Trans.). New York, NY: Continuum.

Gambardella, S. (2020, March 19). *We Are Waves of the Same Sea: COVID-19 and the Philosophy of Unity.* Medium. Retrieved from https://medium.com/the-sophist/we-are-waves-of-the-same-sea-e112b3ade808

LaFrance, A. (2020, June). The Prophecies of Q: American conspiracy theories are entering a dangerous new phase. Retrieved from https://www.theatlantic.com/magazine/archive/2020/06/qanon-nothing-can-stop-what-is-coming/610567/

Madison, D. S. (2010). *Acts of Activism: Human Rights as Radical Performance.* NY: Cambridge University Press.

Pelias, R. (2004). *A Methodology of the Heart: Evoking Academic and Daily Life.* Walnut Creek, CA: AltaMira Press.

Said, E. (1978). *Orientalism.* New York: Random House.

4

THE EMOTIONAL GEOGRAPHIES OF ACADEMIC WRITING: WRITING AS A METHOD OF SURVIVAL

Sophie Tamas, Katarina Georgaras and Maria Dabboussy

Welcome

Come on in! It's so good to see you. Come here, let me give you a hug.

Lament

This paper was lost in the sinking of the old academy, the one where we crammed together in concrete boxes and inhaled one another without fear of anything but scent or stupidity, before campus went down like a great groaning ship while staff and faculty scrambled to build rafts from bits of floating structure so we could pull students in to ride this out.

That paper did not make it. This may not either; we are still adrift. The waves are getting worse and we are already soaked and shivering. In traditional Inuit culture, the grandmothers stayed awake in the igloo through the long winter nights, telling stories and tending the tiny flicker of the oil lamp that was keeping the whole family alive. The grandmother inside me has been murmuring for the past six months, doing what she can to keep me safe and warm.

My lifeboats are held together with shoelaces and require constant bailing so there has been no time to write. The swelling second wave of COVID-19 is crashing upon us now. More than thirty lives were lost in my small town this spring; the coming winter looks like it will be even worse. The living room that used to fill with loved ones has become a playroom for a lonely three-year-old. You, no doubt, have your own wounds that are too sore to touch.

There is a line from Betty Lambert that I like. She was talking about the typical narrative arc of tragedy in theatre, in which a hero who is unfit faces challenges they did not choose and cannot overcome but they persist anyhow. She says,

> I wanted a female tragic form. Women know something that maybe men don't know. We know that after the death, somebody cooks bacon and eggs. And that suicide is not an answer, because life bloody goes on.
>
> *(cited in Wasserman, 1995)*

As I am writing this the leaves outside my window are letting go one by one, fluttering back to where they began. Life is bloody, and going on. I cannot keep your igloo warm, your boat afloat, or my metaphors straight, but *I want to talk about writing out this storm and share the navigational help that I'm getting from emotional geographies.*

I will not do this alone. In dangerous and difficult times we buddy up so that impaired functions (like sense-making and morale) become distributed. Have we ever actually been singular? So I am writing with my students, Maria and Kata, who have both just begun their PhDs in emotional geographies. At the same time, we are beginning a year-long collaborative autoethnographic exploration of feminist scholarly love. This is our launch pad; we're all still feeling shy, so it might be a little awkward.

Emotional Geographies, Served Three Ways

SOPHIE: I have been teaching a graduate seminar on academic emotional geographies for the past four years. This sub-field of human geography draws on affect theory, psychoanalytic theory and feminist geographies (see, for instance, Davidson, Bondi, & Smith, 2016; Lewkowich, 2015; Nunn, 2017; Pile, 2010). It studies the way emotion and affect produce meaning within the body, between bodies, and between bodies, objects and spaces. My students read and talk and then we practice non-rational synthesis through art journaling.

Each week we discuss readings that wrestle with how feeling animates academic practice. I try to make the week on love line up with Valentine's Day, and to alternate difficult with easy feelings. Most of them have read more theory than I have, they're bright and critical and so scared to accidentally do something wrong that they hover on the edge of paralysis. Many have invisible disabilities. I ask them to notice how their bodies respond to the readings. I rarely answer questions but I'll often say, "what you said made me think of…". After we've read and talked, I put out all kinds of art supplies and put a prompt on the board and put on music and we play.

The students talk a lot about anxiety. No matter how good their grades are, they are almost always afraid so we've started studying imposter syndrome as a public feeling that circulates between academic bodies and spaces (Breeze, 2018). We talk about the violent hierarchies and relational toxins in academic environments as well as the joy and love that bring these places to life. I am an autoethnographer, so I teach the way I write, through stories, somewhat shambolic ones that need more structure and less metaphors. I hold the space and encourage them to be kind to themselves.

This is difficult for many of them; it is hard to be kind to yourself while pushing your body into the stress-positions required for academic performances. They depend on our approval and acceptance while we judge and rank them; no wonder there is a mental health crisis in higher education. We discuss what Britzman (2015) calls "the schoolhouse in the mind". I encourage them to throw a party in it, to redecorate, to nail their liberation manifestos to the door. Then I get to watch these brilliant creatures give themselves permission to use all of their senses, to bring more of themselves into connection. I cannot make academic spaces safe but we practice harm reduction. Maybe all I do is love them? Many of my students have never written school work in a voice that they can recognize as their own.

MARIA: Emotional geographies is a lifeline in my journey across academic space through time. Over the years, I have learnt to write traditional literary essays, to research, to cite, to think harshly, with little kindness to authors, and even less kindness to myself as reader and writer. I have learnt to detach from text, and to avoid reading from start to finish. I became a master of tearing arguments apart with smarting words and sharp tongue. Then I stumbled into emotional geography. I could feel the theories and stories breathing life back into my ill academic body, removing fatigue and replacing it with the need to hear and be heard.

Studying and practicing emotional geographies is the rejuvenating experience of listening to your body and mind in relation to yourself, your space and others. My experience with emotional geographies demands my attention and care. In return, emotional geographies lets me bring myself into my studies fully, all of me is welcome in this field. This experience invites loving critique and offers my inherent softness an academic landing space. While I can still feel hurt and angry, and experience discomfort in academia, I do it with care for myself and others. I take the time I need to accept what fills my cup and recognize what is damaging the beautiful experience of the learning process.

KATA: I see emotional geographies as paying attention to feelings and emotions in space and in relation to place. We pay attention to the relational quality of emotions and feelings on a variety of scales from macro to micro.

What I like about emotional geographies as an orienting frame is that it is embodied. I already have all the tools I need to understand emotional geographies; they are inherently in my body. My feelings are not something that

I will be talked out of via theory or philosophy. Though it can be a struggle, I continue to reassert my right to possess my own body, and therefore its ways of knowing and what it feels. I use the word feeling (like Cvetkovich, 2012) because it is imprecise and spans a variety of theoretical definitions of affect and emotion. It also acknowledges the sensory and somatic quality of feelings that are not only cognitive constructions. It speaks to both the embodied as well as psychic or cognitive experiences of emotion and affect. But mostly, it just feels right.

The Emotional Geographies of Writing in the Old Academy

MARIA: I write relationally. Literally. I used to write with my mother, I liked the rush of a looming deadline. I liked smoking cigarettes between bursts of feverish sense making. I liked the darkness and stillness of writing alone in my bed the day before. I would have already written the piece I wanted to submit, but knew even then that submission had more to do with contortion. So I would wait until the night before a deadline, then write all night. The next morning, my mom would scold me. Again? Yes. She would take my hand-written papers, and slowly and gently read them to me while I typed. She would drive me to campus and wait as I printed out my draft. She would do grown-up work on her Blackberry in the car, while I read, edited, then printed again. She would drive me to the next building where I would race up the stairs handing in my assignment just in time. She would have my asthma puffer ready, waiting in the car, because she will always be steps ahead of me. Again and again we would do this dance.

Later, I would write with my sister. My sister who would love me and take care of me during hardship, both hers and mine. My sister who would hear my rasping breath and know the exact time for a kombucha and smoke break. My sister who would read to me with no patience, but all the love in the world. She would tease me for sloppy handwriting but cheer me on for the use of big words and bigger ideas. When we were done, she would smile "you are so smart Maria". I didn't need the grade anymore, and she taught me that I never would again.

Finally, I land. I write with my partner and son. I long for smoke breaks but make do with espresso and earl grey. I draft with my son first, creating a skeleton. Later, I flesh it out to the sound of these beautiful bodies breathing in their sleep. My partner will read to me as I type, he will stumble over my illegible handwriting, over words he has never heard before, and ideas that he does not understand. This will be the only reading or writing he does. He does not enjoy it the way I do, but he does it because he loves my smile and because he cares. Our writing is an act of love for me. I do it because I love myself, and I need to write to make sense of my world. He does it because he loves me and needs me to be sensical. We do it together, but I no longer contort myself for grades. I write what I want. I write for my friends, I stop using big words, but start using more care. I do it with love. I imagine my writing as a cedar tree, rooting itself existentially into the ground, growing slowly, softly, quietly and with strength. Requiring very little from the world, assured in its own resilience. I imagine my son, climbing this tree. I imagine the tree providing shade on a hot day. I imagine a picnic with my mother and sister. I imagine safety and love. I imagine the roots talking to the earth, talking to the other roots. The leaves whisper in the wind calling to all beings that will listen, straining to hear loving whispers back.

KATA: I have rarely, if ever, found joy in academic writing. And I love writing! I write for pleasure, I write for healing, I write for fun, I even write for others! But when I am asked to write a paper it feels like the opposite of joy. It feels like panic: from chronic underlying panic (stiff neck, pressure on my chest) to full-blown panic attacks (taking Clonazopan and lying in bed unable to move).

Let me show you how it feels. This will work best if you happen to be a knitter but should work regardless. Imagine a ball of yarn that has become extremely tangled. You are at a point where you still think that you can untangle this ball of yarn that is the writing, and that untangling it will be annoying, almost painfully so, but ultimately worthwhile. Actually, now that you think of it, this is the last ball of yarn that you have of its type, and you need it to finish the sweater that you've been working on. But this isn't just any sweater. This is a sweater that you're knitting for someone really special in your life. You want to give this sweater to them, so you need to untangle this ball of yarn. See, this person and you haven't spoken in almost 10 years. And now they are on their deathbed, but you think this sweater (and therefore this ball of yarn) is the key to you reconciling before they pass away. So, you don't know if you will be able to untangle this ball of yarn, but you absolutely MUST untangle it, you see?

I'm feeling anxious just thinking about it. Academic writing feels like taking my bleeding, beating, bursting heart and putting it through a meat grinder. It is so fraught with shame that the hot shivers prickle from the top of my head, flush my face and twist my guts. Every paper is a chance for redemption; every paper is opening myself up to rejection. Saying this is embarrassing and shameful. Pathetic but true. I am reliving my childhood every time I sit down to write. Desperately seeking my mother's approval, I am writing to survive.

I use creative writing, lately mostly expressive writing (see Truman, 2016) to manage my feelings. I have overcome this debilitating shame in my creative practice by using the mind tricks that Julia Cameron (1991) taught me in *The Artist's Way*. I tell myself, no one will ever read this. It's going to be bad. I want it to be bad. The worse the better! This is junk, just get out all the junk. And that has helped! I got the junk out and then something else would come out. Or, I'd get the junk out and then realize that it wasn't all junk!

So far, I do not have this experience with academic writing. I know that my profs will read my writing, and then assign a letter grade to it. Grades affect my future. I will not follow that snowball, but you get it, there will be an avalanche, or at least a mountain of snow.

SOPHIE: At first academic writing was a complex skill that I practiced awkwardly and too earnestly. That never stopped, but the face of it changed. When I was younger my papers were portraits of a potential self that I hoped my professors might help me believe into existence. I wrote sentimental poetry and heavy-handed plays and my academic papers were citation puppet-shows. Then in the first year of my PhD I started reading about methods. I found writing as a method of inquiry (Richardson, 2003) and autoethnography (Ellis, 2002). I was able to attend the International Congress of Qualitative Inquiry, where they both were doing workshops. I was bold and they were wise and kind. I was encouraged early and often and still it has taken a very long time for me to stop writing so defensively. It could be that I just found a more compelling act: a kind of written vivisection that made lemonade from my sentimental and dramatic tendencies by theorizing my own trauma.

That's what I would say if I was writing defensively. When I shift out of that voice something I didn't know that I was clenching releases in my chest. Most of the heckling has been coming from me all along. Writing has always been many things: creative writing was my imaginary friend, my stage, my hiding place. Journaling was often a kind of toxic waste tank for things I could neither deal with nor deny. Take elements of both, add overt theory and an audience with generous standards who flip commodified academic writing into an exchange of gifts and you get autoethnography. The tribe who has welcomed me.

The emotional geographies of autoethnography: what does your heart look like? In one of my miserable teenage poems I wrote (god this is embarrassing, isn't that interesting, *why*?) "my heart is a slaughterhouse/hung with the bodies of my loves". I was seventeen, okay? But the line stayed with me because some part of it feels true. Autoethnography works to gradually turn places of death into spaces of care and remembrance. It wraps and buries the bodies and tends to the graves so the spirit can rest. It may visit often. If done well it plants flowers, grows beauty beside loss.

Autoethnography is a quiet space that I hold open with effort, like a bubble of attention in which I listen and sometimes words arrive and I smile to greet them. Hello. Thanks for showing up, I've been missing you. But it's also something I don't know if I've done wrong, if I've been stupid. That feeling is the houseflies in my head – it's what I bring to the writing, not a property of the genre itself. I suppose confident people might feel no such doubts. Or sociopaths. (Valorizing bad habits is a good way to stay stuck.) Muck ruck fuck, just like this paper.

I told you, it's gone and it's not coming back. That future was never going to be and something else is already here. Autoethnography is a monument and a map, a way to say goodbye. I don't want to yet. This is the last year my girls and I will all be at the same university, I thought I had more time to buy them pita dippers and chai in the student union café. More time with loved ones on campus, for full-body hugs in a place that needs them. I am still magically thinking, denying loss. Knowing it does not make it go away. I can't picture the new wonderful, the things I won't be able to imagine living without once I can get up and recalibrate. But the world is not done spinning.

There is a madwoman raving in the attic of this paper. It's a bit overdone, honestly, but how do you judge scale with no horizon? Writing requires a space beside the storm, and produces it, but when things get too wild words scatter. I can just find little scraps, notes written on the backs of price tags and post-its, collected like a little pile of twigs on my desk. It's nothing, it's garbage and whining, but autoethnography says, let me see. I think you might have something there.

Writing is a place I go, a space I inhabit, a helmet I put on, a quiet listening in some interior cavern where thoughts sometimes rustle. I think about it in spatial metaphors – we navigate on narrative journeys, create bridges and scaffolding, stepping stones and pivots. We connect and seek marginalized perspectives. We stall and get stuck. If writing is world-building it is also a geographic practice, one with physical, relational, intellectual, temporal and emotional coordinates.

The emotional geography of academic writing exists for me on several scales. There is the space in my head that I create or visit where writing happens. It is a dark space, sometimes soft, sometimes endless. I wait and listen like a small animal. I can feel the texture of the words as they arrive in my hands, if they are flowing or tacky. Even sweet ones can burn like melted sugar. The flow relies on an alignment or attunement that takes time to thicken; you have to believe it into existence for a long time before it takes form. There's a sensory quality to the words, like a current of air or water that you can ride on but rarely far enough.

It's there again in the relational networks, the shufflings of proximity and distance, trust and critique, security and risk. Who am I close to? This is a spatial question. Autoethnography rearranges the relational furniture. Sometimes it burns down the house – you have to watch yourself. (Madwomen are like that.) It studies and thus inhabits and alters relational spaces. This includes my relations with the avatars of others that exist inside me (not much of you get through). Where do I place you in relation to my mother who does not want to be written about? (Writing that felt like walking on hot sand). In relation to my children? (They showed up at a lectern in Norman Denzin's mouth: I was not expecting that. Where are they now?) My mother is braced against your imaginary judgment; I did that. We are connected to her now, you and I. You did that. Now what do we use this connection for?

Mostly, we have no idea. We are not skilled in connection; we're trained for commodity exchange. In autoethnography you offer your stories, your thoughts about yourself, as a gift. Something given with no expectations calls out in the other a desire to reciprocate (Kimmerer, 2013). If you give me a gift it is distressing to have nothing to give in return. I don't know if this is innate or a result of what my mother might call moral and spiritual education, the actual curriculum of being human (but life is not school; you're not cheating on tests if you find ways to make it easier).

Autoethnography thus produces in the reader a desire to give, and sometimes simultaneously an example of how elusive the bar is for acceptable gifts. Who am I to decide if your gift is worthy? That has to do with the spirit in which it was given. The reader is invited into scenes of mostly normal human crap that everyone takes way too seriously. The fears run around squealing. A coil of desire and dread is the drill that exposes core samples for analysis: hmm, interesting, this trauma fits that pattern. Explain but not ex-pain.

There's the defensive writing again, it's like a tic. I notice it because the writing gets polemic and boring. The texture shifts. If I stop to wonder I see more signs – like that drilling-for-knowledge metaphor. I just critiqued that in my second-year methods course (could you be more phallic?). What I actually mean is that the need for and fear of the other animates my writing like polar charges energize magnetic or electrical fields. When I was younger I ping-ponged between them a lot. I hope to find something like dynamic stillness.

Wounds demand stories, your heart demands stories just like children need stories (because we don't stop being children, we grow around ourselves) and if you listen – if you wait and don't give up on yourself (because the grandma in your igloo would never give up on you) sometimes in the process of self-soothing or sorting things out you write a gift for a reader who feels touched or recognized. You can give something useful. How? Why? Who knows, it makes no sense, you just do it because you can, and then sometimes you receive the sweet baffling gift of a stranger's gratitude.

It connects us, it establishes relationship, because I am here, on the page, trying not to hide. This is what autoethnography allows and demands. Because we break the fourth wall of academic writing the audience must acknowledge relationship with the performer. I see you seeing me. Emotion is not an embarrassing leakage. It still freaks us out, but autoethnographers generally assume it's good for something, worth pondering and welcome to play around our feet as long as it does not ENTIRELY INTERRUPT rational thought. Like, say, a global pandemic plus the crumbling of American democracy. That's a lot of death to process, a lot of fear. A lot of crouching by the back door shivering.

Writing as a Method of Survival for the Pandemic Academic

You would think, if I love autoethnography so much, that I'd be teaching it. I've taught qualitative methods at the second, third and fifth year levels for five years but only began teaching autoethnography this year, since I got tenure. This was not a conscious decision. I have not been excluded for the way that I do scholarship but I still catch myself tiptoeing around the judgments I project onto others.

My cousin is a palliative care physician and a science fiction author. He says since COVID-19 all the medical journals that pooh-poohed narrative are doing special issues of pandemic stories. We need stories when we're afraid; when I'm really in need, I say them out loud. If I can't smell your emotions, if our microbes cannot mingle, our interface is stories. When I talk to you on Zoom you are in pixels and speakers. When I write to you (and I always write to you), you are inside me, a thought. There is nothing closer, you are in my heart. I speak to you as if we could be friends because why would I invite you here in jack boots?

If I understand writing as a spatial practice with relational and imaginary dimensions as well as social and material coordinates, the nature and population of those spaces becomes available for intentional thought. The schoolhouse in the mind is patrolled by what Augusto Boal (1979) called "the cop in the head". If I visualize the headspace where writing happens, I can locate these internal voices. A fear that makes me play safe and small on the page can be traced back to the cop. This gives me leverage; I can recognize that he's trying to protect me. Sometimes I can change the feeling by changing the image. The cop in my head used to be a scornful and disappointed adult standing over me. Now it's a bee in a bell jar. He could be a bouncer that has your back, or a senile patriarch. It is easier to nudge the need than to oppose it. I can also invite safe people in; I can let things advance and recede. I can go there or set it aside.

Mapping the emotional geography of my writing is like reflexivity squared. If stories told by others primarily reveal the rules for speech and thought within the discourses they have available, the stories we tell ourselves about ourselves are no different. I write a lot about how I see myself. By this logic the content of those stories is almost incidental; it's an artifact of what my lifeworld renders speakable. And yet I hang so much moral weight on the ethics of what was said, as if the content could justly be a measure of my worth. These inconsistencies are such a relief, they make me laugh. The cop in my head is just being silly.

The point here for writing for survival is this: maybe the content does not matter as much as the exchange of containers.

KATA: Here is the pep talk I would give myself re: academic writing.

It's ok that you feel very anxious about writing. It's totally understandable. You have been pressured your whole life to perform a set of tricks in order to survive. You were taught to act, speak and write in a certain way in school and you were punished if you resisted. I get it. It's ok. But you're not a child anymore, and you have choices. You are here because you want to be. Actually, you really love most of what you do in school. You even love a lot of the writing process. You love reading, and searching out new ideas, and putting them together like an avant-garde collage. That's all this is. It's just play. It's arts and crafts. You will make many collages. None of them will be perfect, and all of them will contain something worthwhile. But just making the collage (the writing) itself is a radical act of self-love. Just allowing yourself to do something is more than enough. And you'll probably get at least an A – anyway.

This pandemic is kind of giving me a "fuck it" attitude. With so much uncertainty, I feel like there's no status quo to invest in. I see this spilling over into my academic life now. Who knows what will be needed or valued in the future? Who knows what shape the academy will take? This possible (probable) end-of-the-world time is asking me to release whatever I used to believe in terms of being a "good academic". As an underfunded PhD student, I have nothing to lose. It's not like jobs were promised to us when I started grad school. In fact, we were told that it was pretty much a bad idea to do a PhD. Now, not only is there no promise of jobs, but also there is even less promise of a future (at least not one that we can fathom).

This brings me a lot of hope. Maybe the more people are disillusioned by the system; the more opportunities there are for creative intervention. I am leaning in to collaborative writing, potential space and love, as a prayer for the future of academic writing. This is not easy for me; I am constantly worried about letting someone down or that someone is mad at me. I don't always know my boundaries in relation to others and I have some shame about this, but we have to work with what we've got.

We fumble along through trial and error in our real-life relationships. Why should academic work be any different? Let's write our way out of here.

MARIA: In March, as my worlds collided and the floor rushed out beneath my feet, I was too busy to notice that we were already rebuilding. We have all been making cozy nooks. Now I work, study and write on a utilitarian desk that my partner built for me, snuggled between the dining table and our fireplace. As time passes both slowly and swiftly the pandemic has become both the instigator of destruction and a call to redefine community.

We all have a part to play in our collective reckoning. I quarantine while I await my test results. I stay awake all night, my lungs burning in my son's bed with his impossibly small body moaning in his sleep. My partner is in our bedroom, isolating so as not to get sick. I want to be hugged, so I comfort myself with this paper. I sneak downstairs to grab lemon lozenges and orange juice that my mother dropped off on my doorstep. I used to work on campus like this, almost unable to breathe. Socially distanced suffering has pushed kindness and connection to the top of the agenda. Care that cannot be shown is written and sent, and I am filled with gratitude.

I stop saying "when this is over" and start scaffolding and planning. Beginning this PhD is a gift to myself during this pandemic. I write with Kata and Sophie (across emails, in class, in texts, on this paper) and I am grounded each time. I exist this way in this moment, because we exist together. Sophie tells us this is collaborative autoethnography. I add to my reading list (Gale & Wyatt, 2017; Hernandez, Change, & Ngunjiri, 2017) but these are new friends to meet, not tests to pass. I can still access joy even as I forget to breathe. Writing with loved ones is the medicine that I need right now. It offers me a space where I no longer fear talking too much. I don't have time for worrying that I am not doing enough, or doing well enough, and nor do those around me. Mistakes now seem like a natural consequence of our circumstances rather than evidence of my incompetence. I am writing with love, even in school, with permission from emotional geographies. I can no longer write any other way. My aim is to ensure this remains available after the end of the world has come and gone.

What we need now more than ever is low-risk spaces for academic communication in this new digital landscape. How can we translate hugs into words, and keep micro-acts of care from being lost in the floods of other feelings? I want to make these practices palpable and sustaining, not marginalia on the bleak business of being adults. In my work as a departmental administrator I see the necessary kindness, patience, gratitude and support that follows any call for help. This moment is shifting relationships and boundaries to produce portals of care that must be permanently incorporated into the academic landscape. Take a deep breath, this is hard work. In order for us all to survive, we need to lean into the barriers that bind our academic and virtual worlds. The familiar patriarchal, racist, and capitalist walls of academic practice cannot contain or mend bodyminds in distress.

This isolation forces me to examine what I need to thrive, what feels joyful and what harms. I want to hug you and not be afraid. I want to be kind to you and see you reproduce this act of care for yourself and others. I want to write about my feelings, and hear you respond.

Farewell

SOPHIE: All these pivots are making us dizzy (being adrift is like that). We are talking about turning away from writing as a method of excavation and exposure that is meant to manage a hostile world by categorizing the felt as the known and therefore stable – what Sedgewick (2006) would call a doomed paranoid logic – to noticing what is already present and accepting it. Not necessarily liking or endorsing but accepting, if only because it is already here.

The Biblical framing of human knowledge as a spiteful divine gift still echoes through our not-so-secular academic structures, making it seem normal to experience the acquisition of knowledge as punishment and exile. Neoliberalism doubles down by cultivating individual employability rather than connection and exploration. The interdependency we are pointing out does not live in some contrary discursive ether that we are hoping to enact; it is embedded in the world (Anderson & Harrison, 2010). The mind, so long seen as a uniquely human blessing/curse, may in fact arise from any networked system that reaches sufficient complexity. Listen to Levin and Dennett (2020):

> The key dynamic that evolution discovered is a special kind of communication allowing privileged access of agents to the same information pool, which in turn made it possible to scale selves. This kickstarted the continuum of increasing agency.

They argue that the cells and tissues in our body act as agents with agendas, and that they (along with swarms or collectives of other things at various scales) achieve this through communication which allows for cooperation and localized decision-making. Agency emerges from collectives. Losing contact has dire consequences:

> ...preventing this physiological communication within the body – by shutting down gap junctions or simply inserting pieces of plastic between tissues – initiates cancer, a localised reversion to an ancient, unicellular state in which the boundary of the self is just the surface of a single cell and the rest of the body is just 'environment' from its perspective, to be exploited selfishly.

Hello, neoliberal subjectivity. But wait! There's more!

> And we now know that artificially forcing cells back into bioelectrical connection with their neighbours can normalise such cancer cells, pushing them back into the collective goal of tissue upkeep and maintenance....An important implication of this view is that cooperation is less about genetic relatedness and much more about physiological interoperability. As long as the hardware is good enough to enable physiological communication of this type, the exact details aren't nearly as important...Remarkably, the physiological software isn't 'hardwired' or even 'firmware'; these gap junctions have – like synapses – a memory, and are affected by prior states of the cells. (no page numbers).

As long as the hardware is good enough to enable physiological communication: I call that a rubric.

In a beautiful Zoom conference session this summer Bryant Keith Alexander shared the beautiful thought that genius resides in the community, not in the individual. This makes sense, as all sense-making emerges from discourses that are collectively built. He was citing someone whose name I never quite caught, but I thank them for this thought. It tells me that writing is useful so long as it builds community, because this is how we create the conditions in which our complex networked system – our collective mind – gathers agency. The nature or impact of that agency depends on the content and weave of the network. Writing to connect requires being as present as possible on the page and inviting the reader to come close enough to touch. This does not mean being nice or naive about everything; touch can hurt. Hope is difficult. It requires trust. But we're here anyhow; we might as well lean into it.

In rough waters with no land in sight you lash your boats together. I've got Maria and Kata and they've got me. Now you do, too. Hello. What a storm, hey? Like a tsunami it might leave our communities unrecognizable but there is a quiet sustaining murmur beyond the cold walls of our separation.

References

Anderson, B., & Harrison, P. (2010). The promise of non-representational theories. In B. Anderson & P. Harrison (Eds.), *Taking place: Non-representational theories and geography* (pp. 1–34). Farnham, UK: Ashgate Publishing.

Boal, A. (1979). *Theatre of the oppressed* (C. & M.-O. L. McBride, Trans.). New York: Urizen.

Breeze, M. (2018). Imposter syndrome as a public feeling. In Y. Taylor & K. Lahad (Eds.), *Feeling academic in the neoliberal university: Feminist flights, fights and failures* (pp. 191–215). London: Palgrave.

Britzman, D. (2015). Between psychoanalysis and pedagogy: Scenes of rapprochement and alienation, *Curriculum Inquiry*, 43(1), 95–117.

Cameron, J. (1991). *The artist's way: a spiritual path to higher creativity*. New York: J.P. Tarcher/Putnam.

Cvetkovich, A. (2012). Depression is ordinary: Public feelings and Saidiya Hartman's *Lose Your Mother. Feminist Theory*, *13*(2), 131–146. DOI: 10.1177/1464700112442641.

Davidson, J., Bondi, L., & Smith, M. (2016). *Emotional geographies*. Hampshire, UK: Ashgate.

Ellis, C. (2002). Being real: Moving inward toward social change. *Qualitative Studies in Education, 15*(4), 399–406.

Gale, K., & Wyatt, J. (2017). Working at the wonder: Collaborative writing as a method of inquiry. *Qualitative Inquiry, 23*(5), 355–364.

Hernandez, K. C., Change, H., & Ngunjiri, F. W. (2017). Collaborative Autoethnography as Multivocal, Relational, and Democratic Research: Opportunities, Challenges, and Aspirations. *a/b: Auto/Biography Studies, 32*(2), 251–254. DOI: 10.1080/08989575.2017.1288892.

Kimmerer, R. W. (2013). *Braiding sweetgrass: Indigenous wisdom, scientific knowledge, and the teachings of plants*. Minneapolis, MN: Milkweed.

Levin, M., & Dennett, D. C. (2020). Cognition all the way down. In N. Warburton (Ed.), *Aeon Essays*.<aeon.co/essays/How to Understand Cells, Tissues and Organisms as Agents with Agendas>.

Lewkowich, D. (2015). Reminders of the abject in teaching: Psychoanalytic notes on my sweaty, pedagogical self. *Emotion, Space and Society, 16*, 41–47.

Nunn, N. (2017). Emotional and relational approaches to masculine knowledge. *Social & Cultural Geography, 18*(3), 354–370.

Pile, S. (2010). Emotions and affects in recent human geography. *Transactions of the Institute of British Geographers, 35*, 5–20.

Richardson, L. (2003). Writing: A method of inquiry. In N. K. Denzin & Y. S. Lincoln (Eds.), *turning points in qualitative research: Tying knots in a handkerchief* (pp. 379–396). Walnut Creek, CA: AltaMira.

Sedgewick, E. (2006). Teaching/Depression. *The Scholar & Feminist Online, 4*(2), 1–6.

Truman, S. E. (2016). Becoming more than it never (actually) was: Expressive writing as research-creation. *Journal of Curriculum and Pedagogy, 13*(2), 136–143.

Wasserman, J. (1995). Daddy's girls: Father-daughter incest and Canadian plays by women. *Essays in Theatre, 14*, 24–36.

5

IT IS A LONELY VOICE BETWEEN SOCIAL REBELLION AND THE PANDEMIC

César A. Cisneros Puebla

Creative subversion as a research object is a process that generates interest in researchers who study nonviolent actions against rules and that serve to negotiate the social construction of social orders. Such actions are transformative and can emerge individually or collectively in different social arenas. Creative subversion is basically a rational act that evolves the actant human being with all its emotional and subjective forces.

As I have discussed before (Cisneros, 2020b), subversive acts are labeled by other actors who do not act in the same way. The subversive is discursively constructed because another actant has labeled with words the act that received such description. Or, could we think that acts of creative subversion are ontologically subversive in themselves? Or, is the quality of subversion acquired through the form that is assigned by others and is therefore relational? In this way, being subversive and acting subversively creative is historically located in the discursive practices of the social space, arena, or institution in which it occurs. Since the subversive is historically situated, it can be naturalized as normal and obvious, which in the past could have been rejected and excluded for altering the order.

When subversive acts occur at the individual level, the optics of analysis are usually taken to the field of genius or madness. Revolutionary acts are also seen, evaluated, and sometimes isolated by social forces that seek to prevent their evolution. Genius in the individual is usually separated only by a very fine thread of stupidity or imbecility. If they are not expelled and ostracized, individuals with creative genius can generate collective movements. On the contrary, when subversive acts happen at the collective level, they are not analyzed as collective genius; the genius condition applies only to individuals, not to masses or crowds. For instance, the collective process of creative subversion during civil insurrection can be performed by writing, painting, sculpting, graffitiing, marching, protesting, shouting, screaming, singing, playing music, doing new thing with useless old thing, doing activism, and so on. Each of these different ways of acting has received different attention from the human and social sciences. It is worth mentioning, for example, the efforts of Fotaki and Daskalaki (2020), Curnow, Davis and Asher (2019), and Apoifis (2017) in regards of activism; on collaborative writing it is worth mentioning Gale and Wyatt (2012), Bogdanich (2014), and Gale et al. (2019) just to provide some authors to follow in the directions and approaches they are pointed out.

It is imperative to promote anywhere in the world the creative process of generating meanings, practices, actions, performances, objects, paintings, sculptures, or anything to question the order of discursive domination, whether in the family, institutional, sexual, social, economic, or political sphere. As an individual or collective effort, it can produce a schism in the social architecture of the domain, be it in artistic, musical, political, or social spheres or wherever. Resisting has become, since the modern times of Charles Baudelaire and Charlie Chaplin as prototypical cases, a necessary position for social change. The other Charlie, the one from the 21st century, surnamed Hebdo, is now also an icon of resistance.

Resistance is always a preamble to creative subversion: It occurs at the individual and/or collective levels. When civic resistance occurs anywhere in the world, it is an opportune time to participate as a qualitative researcher to ethnographically describe and interpret social rebellion and indignation worldwide. Beyond the political and epistemological crisis that ethnography was experiencing towards the end of the last century (Clifford & Marcus, 1986), I believe we can experiment with new forms of writing (Goodall, 2000). I firmly believe that creative subversion is a politically oriented methodological approach that is allied with the subaltern classes and aims to destroy the current social and ideological hegemonies and to generate new social harmonies. From historical perspective, it has deep roots in the Situationist International movement as we have already shown above but also in certain political criticism that was formulated in the 1980s from Marxism (Negri, 2005). In this context, the researcher cannot simply witness what is happening in the world, since the aim of ethnographers is not only to testify, as Bochner (2000) and Denzin (2017) have critically shown. We can transform ourselves into a voice that screams, into a theater that dramatizes, into an activist that investigates, into a researcher protesting, into a box that resounds, with the poetics of anger that exist throughout the world. That is the methodology of creative subversion.

Below I offer a brief inventory of characteristics (Cisneros, 2020b) of creative subversion taken as a research object:

- Any free artistic expression that exceeds the limits of its time.
- Every dramatization that critically recreates the communicative construction of the world.
- Any act whose purpose is to eliminate inequality between human beings.
- Every action that unveils and makes visible the networks of social control and political dominance.
- Those acts that produce new meaning where there was none before.
- Any act whose purpose is to build a loving world.
- Every act that produces a broad sense of hope for social change.
- Any act that denounces injustices and creates ways to eliminate them.
- Any act of protest, any act of rebellion, any act of love.
- Any act to build new understandings and to mobilize new subjectivities.
- Those acts that launch a different way of feeling, acting, and thinking.
- Any act whose purpose is to eliminate the orders that legitimize social injustice.
- All those acts that inspire others to participate in processes of social transformation.
- Any action that produces the extension of civic resistance.
- Every action that humorously destabilizes any established order.
- Any act whose purpose is to eliminate oppression from the face of our planet.
- Any act questioning the current order of dominance.
- Any act whose purpose is to build an ecologically sustainable world.
- All those acts that structurally transform the daily life of the wretched.
- Any action that produces rebellion against power.

Creative subversion has different expressions and can be seen as anger, rage, or simply rebellion. From the sociological tradition of conflict (see, e.g., Collins, 1994), we would identify any disorder as a promoter of change: even more so if it is a change caused by conflict of social classes. For such reasons, all these expressions of social and political conflicts are generally believed to be destructive: unpleasant, immature, aggressive, hostile, antisocial, impulsive, abominable, illicit, and indecent emotions. We know that conservative thinkers put these labels on any expression that suggests a minimal degree of creative subversion, even if there were a degree of zero.

Would it be possible to divide qualitative inquiry into that which is interested in studying social order and that which is interested in studying social conflict? If the answer is affirmative, I must declare that my position is not only to study social conflict but also to stand myself on the side of the actors who provoke subversion. Subversiveness is a state of mind and a materiality. There are other researchers who I believe share this position. Regarding free artistic expressions qualitative researchers have already explored literature, poetry, theater, performances, painting, comedy, music, and so on to present the findings of their inquiry. It may be called visionary activism (Faulkner, 2017) and be applied not only to poetry, for example. Such new ways of spreading and/or disseminating research findings have been creating new meaning where there was none before.

We can also recognize efforts in qualitative inquiry linked to the construction of social justice with a broad sense of hope for social change (Denzin & Giardina, 2009). When we are collaborating in civil resistance movements, popular riots, urban intervention projects, and ecological transformation, for human rights and gender equality, or working alongside the wretched and dispossessed, we are building critical qualitative inquiry in the form of militant ethnography as practiced by Fotaki and Daskalaki (2020), Curnow, Davis and Asher (2019), and Apoifis (2017).

An Invisible Enemy When the Human Enemy Is Invincible

The year 2020 is and will be remembered as a very meaningful one. It is a year that combines – as never seen before – apocalyptic visions, conspiracy theories, fake news, and horrendous scenes for the future after the coronavirus pandemic. Since the very beginning, news was so alarming that necropolitics (Mbembe, 2003) became a popular term amid any collective concern about the health policies created around the world. Theoretical ideas about the cyclical crisis of capitalism were also on everyone's lips again remembering the beginning of 1929 recession and the total deaths caused by Spanish Flu since 1918.

Chile has a place in the world: It is the country in which the most liberal economic policies have been implemented, taking place the most spectacular free market experiment, together with the United Kingdom. Such an experiment began with the massacre that ended the socialist regime of President Salvador Allende, who was democratically elected in 1970. On September 11, 1973, with a criminal coup, Pinochet began one of the most horrible terrorist dictatorships in human history. Military dictatorship that ended in 1990 to give way to a "concerted democracy" that is actually a civil dictatorship that has had Aylwin, Frei, Lagos, and Bachelet as presidents. Nowadays this civil dictatorship it is headed by Sebastián Piñera. In the last 30 years (1990–2020), Chile has been named as "Chilean way of life" for the migrants, in reference to the "American way of life" for other migrants; or "oasis" in the midst of convulsed South America. Jara-Labarthé and Cisneros Puebla (in press) have analyzed the situation of immigrants to Chile as a vulnerable population during the emergency produced by the COVID-19 pandemic. Cisneros (2020a) has produced an interpretation of the Chilean social rebellion recently started in October 18,

2020. Such an interpretation is based on the analysis of social conflict as a drama. Poetics of rage is the focus of such interpretation to recreate the meaning changes of any objects used in the social protest. The subversiveness of any materiality is interpreted as an object of qualitative inquiry.

The following piece was written on April 29, 2020, as a reflective exercise of qualitative inquiry to share with collaborative writing colleagues. It is inspired by the methodology of subversive creativity and I wish to present it as a brief and humble contribution and it is one more episode of the personal narrative about the Chilean drama of the popular rebellion in its connection with the COVID-19 pandemic from the perspective of love as resistance. A first version was posted to the Emotional Geographies Lab at Carleton University, Canada, on May 4, 2020.[1] It has been expanded, corrected, improved, enjoyed, updated, shared, and rewritten.

INSIDE-OUTSIDE

Pandemic is isolation
Living without permission to enjoy the streets
To be without being
What is going on outside?
It rains and I cannot enjoy it
Sunny day with no people on the streets

Pandemic is inhumanity
War without a specific enemy[2]
Is an illusion only what I live?

But I am happy, after all
Well I have life only between four walls with a person I love
Although I cannot go for a walk without permission from the military

Finally living in Chile is like living in dictatorship
A government that murdered young students just a few months ago
A deep popular rebellion was happening in the streets when this virus
    appeared
And now we cannot go out

But I am happy in the end
Well I have life only between four walls with a person I love
Although I cannot go for a walk without permission from the military

But … is it only an illusion that I live?
What if it is a dream and everything remains the same?
Does living in confinement make you happy? What madness…what madness!!
Outside nothing exists
Outside nothing exists

Only inside is life
Between my four walls
Barricades have another meaning today

Nothing is happening outside
In Chile, the pandemic defeated a popular rebellion
And President Piñera choose another enemy, now microscopic

Being blind
Piñera look at the microscopic
while living in his parallel universe… his personal oasis

While destroying his human enemy with military weapons
to his microscopic enemy he respectfully asks to withdraw
He lives in a ritualized world
He lives in a world populated by virus
He communicates with the viruses
He speaks to them

Covid19 has shown us the true enemies against the light
Public health policies
Some ignorant Presidents
Our centuries of shattered humanity

But I am happy, after all
Well I have life only between four walls with a person I love
Although I cannot go for a walk without permission from the military

Only inside is life
Between my four walls
Barricades have another meaning today

Piñera is like the other Presidents
of other countries
those who fight against COVID-19 only with prayers
and religious stamps

Finally living in Chile is like living in dictatorship
A government that murdered young students just a few months ago
Chilean citizens have a President that ask to Coronavirus
"leave us alone and leave the country"

A government that murdered young students just a few months ago
And have a President that ask the Coronavirus
"leave us alone and leave the country"

At the end…
Pandemic is inhumanity

Notes

1 This original version can be accessed here https://carleton.ca/emogeolab/2020/inside-outside/.
2 Visiting the small town I live in (no more than 240,000 inhabitants), President Piñera on August 29, 2020, said, referring to National priorities: "…Unfortunately, they changed because of a microscopic and invisible virus, but lethal and very destructive, called coronavirus, and I ask you, as President of Chile, to leave us alone and leave the country…" (See: https://www.archynewsy.com/pinera-calls-for-the-coronavirus-and-asks-to-leave-us-alone-and-leave-the-country-national/)

References

Apoifis, N. (2017). Fieldwork in a furnace: Anarchists, anti-authoritarians and militant ethnography. *Qualitative Research*, *17*(1), 3–19.

Bochner, A. (2000). Criteria against ourselves. *Qualitative Inquiry*, *6*, 266–272.

Bogdanich, J. (2014). The (cue) spaces between: Teaching Shakespeare and collaborative writing. *Cultural Studies-Critical Methodologies*, *14*(4), 380–384.

Cisneros Puebla, C. (2020a). Poetics of rage as performative creative subversion: Autoethnography and social drama. In N. Denzin & J. Salvo (Eds), *New Directions in Theorizing Qualitative Research: Performance as Resistance* (pp. 103–113). Gorham, ME: Myers Education Press.

Cisneros Puebla, C. (2020b). Creative subversion: Staking a claim for critical qualitative inquiry. *Qualitative Inquiry*. Retrieved from https://journals.sagepub.com/doi/10.1177/1077800420933298

Clifford, J., & Marcus, G. (1986). *Writing Culture. The Poetics and Politics of Ethnography*. Berkeley and Los Angeles: University of California Press.

Collins, R. (1994). *Four Sociological Traditions*. Oxford: Oxford University Press.

Curnow, W., Davis, A., & Asher, L. (2019). Politicization in process: Developing political concepts, practices, epistemologies, and identities through activist engagement. *American Educational Research Journal*, *56*(3), 716–752.

Denzin, N. (2017). Critical qualitative inquiry. *Qualitative Inquiry*, *23*, 8–16.

Denzin, N., & Giardina, M. (2009). *Qualitative Inquiry and Social Justice: Toward a Politics of Hope*. Walnut Creek, CA: Left Coast Press.

Faulkner, S. (2017). Poetry is politics: An autoethnographic poetry manifesto. *International Review of Qualitative Research*, *10*(1), 89–96.

Fotaki, M., & Daskalaki, M. (2020). Politicizing the body in the anti-mining protest in Greece. *Organization Studies*. Retrieved from https://journals.sagepub.com/doi/10.1177/0170840619882955

Gale, K., & Wyatt, J. (2012). Back to futures: Diffractions and becomings of collaborative writing. *International Review of Qualitative Research*, *5*(4), 467–477.

Gale, K., Wyatt, J., Gullion, J., Hou, N., Jeansonne, C., Linnell, S., Reaves, M., Reilly, R., & Rhodes, P. (2019). Deleuze and collaborative writing in the dance of activism. *International Review of Qualitative Research*, *12*(3), 323–338.

Goodall, H. L. (2000). *Writing the New Ethnography*. Walnut Creek, CA: AltaMira Press.

Jara-Labarthé, V., & Cisneros Puebla, C. (in press). Migrants in Chile: Social crisis and the pandemic (or sailing over troubled water…). *Qualitative Social Work*.

Mbembe, A. (2003). Necropolitics. *Public Culture*. *15*(1): 11–40.

Negri, A. (2005). *The Politics of Subversion: A Manifesto for the Twenty-first Century*. Cambridge: Polity Press.

6

WHIMSY, ETHNOGRAPHIC WRITING, AND THE EVERYDAY: POSSIBILITIES, POLITICS, POETICS

Katie Fitzpatrick and Jonathan Wyatt

Introduction: Waving at a Passing Train

In her 2015 paper, *Towards a Politics of Whimsy: Yarn Bombing in the City,* Joanna Mann argues for whimsy's capacity to prompt change. Impossible to grasp, always in excess, always in–between, whimsy, she argues, is "intrinsically joyous" (p. 65), a way of becoming in the world that renders the familiar, the quotidian, indeterminate, and mysterious and that calls the body into action. "Despite, or perhaps because of, its out-of-placeness", Mann writes, "whimsy can function as a powerful political force that is able to … foster new ethical spaces and modes of political action" (p. 65).

★★★

Katie, December 16, 2019

I'm driving home from work, along my usual route. The day has been filled with meetings, emails, plans for next year. As ever, I try to focus on academic writing and get consumed, instead, by admin. It consumes me, eats me whole, swallows my day. I'm thinking about this as I drive, winding along roads lined with summer trees. The route I take to get home from work includes a railway crossing. As I approach it, the lights flash and the barrier arm swings down. This happens often. I don't mind this pause in the journey. It makes me happy to see the train and to know that this city is getting more committed to public transport. I think about my own driving, and feel a little ashamed about the choices I make to get to work. A blue car is stopped in front of me, the only one between me and the train, which is now approaching the crossing, moving towards the city. As the train rushes closer, the driver of the blue car extends his arm out of the window and starts waving. He keeps waving and waving, arm extended to its full length, an insistent and enthusiastic wave. He waves to each carriage without stopping. He keeps waving and waving until the train is past. Until the lights and bells subside, until the pause is over and the day is resumed. Once I notice him waving I watch the train, each carriage filled with people going somewhere. And not one single person waves back. I watch the whole scene with a mixed sense of wonder (will he keep waving, why is he waving? who is he waving to?) and tension (will someone wave back? how long will he keep waving for?). I am answered soon enough: he kept waving for the whole passing of the train. No one waved back. At first, I feel a bit sad. Surely someone might have waved, returned his gesture, made a connection? But then I realize that the waving back doesn't matter; his waving was an action sent forth, a gesture that is not diminished by a lack of reciprocity. His waving didn't require any such obvious or spontaneous validation.

The wave is like a poem that we send out into the world and we don't know what response, if any, it will get. We don't know what effect, if any, it will have.

★★★

In this chapter, we think, write and play with notions of whimsy, drawing into our scrutiny and inquiry reflections on how whimsy intersects our everyday living and working. We follow whimsy in exploring ways of doing and being in the world, in the academy, and in inquiry. We seek to catch up with how whimsy stretches us: whimsy as engaged, gritty, relational, political encounter, an ethico-onto-epistemological something-that-happens. Waving at a passing train from a car obliged to stop is relational, powerful; a moment of potential contact offered into the busy-ness of an early-evening rush hour, a gesture whose effects are open; a summons into the unknown.

We could position this paper within substantive scholarly fields, for example as an argument within discourses about mental health and the potentialities of whimsy (e.g., Williams & Doessel, 2018). We could rehearse previous arguments about neoliberalism and the constraints of the academy and why we need whimsy especially right now, especially when we are locked down, locked out, and have restricted geographical possibilities (e.g., Davies, Gottsche, & Bansel, 2006). We could position whimsy in instrumental ways as "important", "useful", "meeting a need", "filling a gap". We could, but we won't. We won't, because to attempt to do so misses whimsy, fails to pay attention. Whimsy resists being tied down to the logics of those kinds of argument.

Instead, we offer a text that attempts to pay due respect to whimsy's ontology and to what whimsy can teach us. We engage with writing that came to us between June 2019 and August 2020 as we were living and working (Katie in Auckland, New Zealand; Jonathan in Edinburgh, United Kingdom), and, until March 2020, when we were travelling; when travelling was possible, taken for granted, privileged, and when it was possible to be with others, go to cafés and bars, hug, leave our home cities. The writing also turns to how we each have been living through the COVID-19 pandemic, and its implications and politics. The chapter's writing moves between these times. The writing is exploratory, jarring, incommensurate; exchanges across continents, across chronological time, and across time zones, as we search for whimsy and what it teaches us. We draw on writing from the fields of ethnography, poetic inquiry, and qualitative writing (Lather, 2007; Richardson, 2000, 2004), showing rather than telling what might be possible if we attend to whimsy in our writing.

Whimsy and What Counts

Jonathan, June 2020

I wonder what counts as whimsical during a pandemic. Maybe not the cold, unwelcome breeze as I sit outside on this bench on a late mid-summer evening, nor the rare, obtrusive car rattling over the cobbles. Nor the nagging awareness of pain in my body. But maybe the grey underbelly of the clouds as they blow east overhead. Maybe the blackbird singing on a nearby roof, audible only when the car has passed. Maybe sitting here, being here, on this bench, my favorite city bench near home. Maybe writing here in this notebook.

Or maybe the show I watched earlier, the actors performing themselves being actors thwarted by the virus, rehearsing online a play whose rehearsals and performances have been cancelled; the impact on livelihoods, cultural life, life, lives, all, hinted at through the humor and pathos of their futile venture. Maybe singing 91st birthday greetings to Mum through my phone and the phone being held by her carer, Elsa, whom I have never met. Maybe Mum's face, happy with the surprise and confusion. Maybe the light drops of rain falling on me now. Maybe the pandemic quiet itself, this city stillness.

Katie, January 2020

Walking on the beach, on holiday, on the east coast of Aotearoa, New Zealand. It is remote here, out of bounds. Off grid. There is 1 bar of service on my cell phone. If I walk around I can sometimes get 2 bars, but it's inconsistent. Being on holiday feels whimsical. Writing about whimsy feels indulgent, like it could be purposeless. Like it could be tangential. Tangential to what? To the kind of writing I usually do: argumentative, certain, purposeful, political.

As I walk, I see a small, dried, star-like, circular plant – I guess it's a dried seed head – tumbling across the sand. I take a short video of it. The only visible thing moving on the beach, that I can see. That I notice. But the beach is, of course, full of life and movement and action. Holes in the sand signal creatures underneath; their breathe-holes. The waves move incessantly, rhythmically but unpredictably, crashing, moving up and back, across and awash, tumbling so that my small dog runs away.

Jonathan, February 2020

I'm traveling by train, south through Italy, a full day from Milan to Siracusa, Sicily, on my way to Malta for the 2020 European Congress of Qualitative Inquiry. Back in Edinburgh I have been feeling small, remote from myself; I have been tumbling, blown across the sand. The train spears south along the west coast, rocks, and ocean staccato-glimpsed between tunnels.

I'm unwell. Not seriously. Well, yes, seriously, in that it's not funny, it's miserable. But not critically. Well, yes, "critically" in the scholarly sense that it's throwing me into and against the material-discursive constructions of how the medical world characterizes "illness". I read Arthur Frank again, having first read him at a distance 10 years ago, but now I'm in, I am, his text. He's writing about me, a wounded storyteller veering between the *recovery* and *chaos* narratives and mostly unable to access the *quest* narrative. So, let's say I'm unwell and it's critical, but it's not life-threatening. No, that's not right either: it's a threat to who I am, how I see myself. I tumble as the not-being-well arrives in waves, comes, and goes, crashing upon me, unpredictable.

The journey south takes me through Florence and Rome, and along the west coast, the line hewn through rock and hugging beaches. I arrive in Siracusa late. Early next morning, I look for the train at Siracusa that will take me to Pozzallo and the ferry to Valletta. I wander the station, the information board directing me to a platform I can't find. After 15 minutes of fruitless searching I ask for guidance from the man staffing the desk, pointing at my ticket. He directs me to the back of the station, away from the main lines. I find a lone, abandoned carriage, its shell decorated – or defaced, depending upon your point of view – by the multiple vivid colors and swirls of spray-painted graffiti. I wonder why the authorities leave it there, why they haven't junked it. I'm early, so wait on a bench nearby. Another passenger arrives, and another. They pass me by and alight the abandoned carriage.

When still others arrive and do the same, it becomes clear this decorated, abandoned carriage is not junk: it's my train. I jump on and, soon after, we leave. Hope is there, I sense, its life, movement, and action in the surprising speed of a psychedelic train carriage; hope is alive, its breath brushing my cheek through open windows.

★★★

Whimsy may be something that surprises on the way home from work, like a man waving at a train; something not planned that interrupts the purpose of the evening, that makes us think about the futility of arbitrary practices. How such practices are imposed, insisted upon. It is awareness of the arbitrary practices of necessity. The whimsical interrupts our focus on the banal, the practical, the instrumental. Whimsy is the oblique, it is refusal, it is resistance to conforming. It's the graffiti-sprayed carriage whose value we don't see. It is responsiveness to that which is (apparently) invisible, the tumbling seed head we notice that calls us to that which we ignore. It's stopping where a steep, wide path curves right, to notice white butterflies that can barely be seen. It's the autumn sun, cool-warm on the skin. It is the thing out of place (a rose on the pavement, a magnolia inexplicably in full bloom in the winter grey); and/or unexpected – a bright red velvet coat, a downpour as you're getting out of the car without an umbrella; an art work a colleague slides under our door one morning (photos from an exhibition for her late husband) to say "thank you for listening". It is a surprise that makes us smile but, more than that, it's a surprise that throws the arbitrary into perspective. It does something. Whimsy is less that which is out of place and more what may be deeply in and of place, necessary, the necessary we fail (most times) to notice, and that reminds us of beauty, fragility, mortality, connection.

Whimsy is the poetic, not as tangential or as distraction, but the poetic as a reminder of what counts, of what matters.

This is not a poem

This is not a poem. This is not a poem as it has sentences, like this one; and capital letters; and full stops, like that first one back there after "poem"; and this one about to appear, here. It even has semi-colons, as you can see. It can't be poem.

This is not a poem. This is rebel prose, its full lines, proper paragraphs, and multiple prepositions taking a stand against the spare and the implicit. No hints, no nuance, no paring back when you read this. No hidden meanings here.

This is not a poem. It's not about feeling. Poems are about feeling, about the moving heart, the moved heart; about the body's depths, the blood coursing. They're about fire. Pain. Loss. Joy. Hope. Love. (Did you see that? The sentences shorten and, lo, the poetic appears.)

This is not a poem. It has sentences, capital letters, punctuation, is without hidden meanings, and is not about feeling. This is not a poem; it never will be. This is full prose. Delight, longing, desire, loss, love; none of these lies hidden between these lines. It's not, and never will be, a poem; its words, phrases, full sentences and plentiful punctuation marks will never be stuttering gestures of touch and glimpses of, hope for, what is possible.

Listening with Whimsy

Katie, January 2020

For my own work, in school ethnography (e.g., Fitzpatrick, 2013), whimsy helps me to let go of the direct question, the focused inquiry. It lets me just be in the field (or whatever a research context might be called) and just be open to what's happening, what's not happening, what speaks, what might be surprising. Whimsy is actually everywhere if you are open to it (but not looking for it). I think of it rather as "listening with your whimsy". You can hear and attend to things that are there but which might be (almost) imperceptible.

> *Here is a recording of the ocean*
> *you will hear the waves*
> *Loud and insistent*
> *A force of collision, resounding*
> *dominating*
> *answering the direct question*
> *but, if you listen carefully*
> *you can hear my breathing*
> *and the tussock waving in the wind*
> *If you listen with your whimsy*
> *you can hear*
> *the memory of oyster catchers flying overhead*
> *a bee grazing a flower*
> *the edge of a butterfly arc*
> *the death that resides in each moment*
> *the tail of the wind*

It's easy, perhaps to listen for whimsy on holiday but what about when I'm researching, doing ethnographic work in school, caught up in the pressures of academia, schooling logics, systems that frame possibilities? What then? When I read back to my ethnographic writing in a school in 2016, I can sense whimsy there too:

> I feel the deep dragging pull of the school timetable. The inflexibility of the day that my body rebels against. When the alarm goes off in the morning, I immediately start bargaining with myself, I try to make excuses and then castigate myself for such weakness. I remember this feeling as a teacher (not so much as a student); my body is recalling the ache of days on end of routine, the lethargy I felt at crossing the days off the calendar as they stretched endlessly through winter. It's not that I didn't enjoy teaching in high schools; I actually loved it, I was highly motivated and worked hard (too hard), but I always felt the routine, timetable, and set-nature of the school day invoked a certain inertia. My body resists the endless stretch

of time on the calendar and I start counting the days. Right now, I am sitting in a year 12 health education class and counting the weeks until the school holidays when I can re-embrace the flexible time I usually live as an academic. The funny thing is though, there are few expectations on me here as a researcher. Although all interactions are performative, I have little in the way of planned performance to enact here. And maybe that's part of the problem: my role is an ambivalent one and I don't feel very useful to the school on a day to day basis. I am hovering, lingering, asking questions and just hanging out and writing. I think if I had microphones on students, was measuring interactions or had a rubric for teaching and learning then it would be more obvious. I would have 'hard data' to present to the school. What I have so far are long, written reflections on classes, snatches of conversations, my thoughts and feelings about the school, and recorded research conversations. Last week someone asked me what I was finding. I just replied: 'it's too early to know'.

Germs

In the classrooms all I can think of is
Germs
snot, body fluids, dried blood, spit
I get sick three times in two months
soaking up the germs, taking them into my body
Students ache their way to school, filled with flu
trudge-walking heavy cold corridors
trying to listen through headache haze
shivering in the back of the room
I imagine the germs on the surfaces that never get cleaned
I can see them float in the humid heated air
I can smell them on the windows

Revisiting this makes me think about several things. First, that ethnographic methods are themselves whimsical. Or, they at least require a suspension of the organized, purposeful, and direct search for meaning. Ethnographic work requires us to be open, bored, uncertain, patient, enduring, responsive. It requires us to experience without assuming particular meanings. It is possible – even ideal – to undertake ethnographic work and not be really sure what you're looking for, what you're sensing, what might be experienced. It is common to feel off track, to assume what's happening isn't relevant, to feel lost. Lather (2007) describes getting lost as an ontological necessity, in moving towards ethnographic "research approaches that no longer confidently assume that we are 'in the know'" (p. 4). She suggests that researchers might purposely get lost "at the limits of representation" and engage in "a fruitful sense of dislocation in our knowledge projects" (p. 4). When I began the above ethnography, I was interested (I thought) in health education pedagogies in schools. I was interested in the curriculum and in student experiences. I never anticipated the sickness my own body would experience, how that would limit my willingness to be at school, how I might see schools in relation to physical health. I did feel lost doing ethnographic work, lost and unsure, and bored and lethargic. Denzin (2015, p. 200) reminds us that "Meanings are always in motion, incomplete, partial, contradictory". Accepting this, seeking this, is whimsical practice.

Jonathan, August 15, 2020

It's a Saturday. I've been alone all my day thus far. I have spoken with myself, had conversations with others within me, had text exchanges, written an email to a friend. I've listened to the news – the reimposed quarantine on travelers to parts of Europe, Auckland's extended lockdown, the thrashing of Barcelona in the remaining European Champions League games. An 8-2 loss to Bayern Munich, but with no one there to witness it in person, I wonder who cares. I try to care, I am open to the usual excitement, but find none.

Words have surrounded me today, have circulated within me, but I haven't spoken aloud to anyone, except to order coffee at Soderberg in nearby Stockbridge. I was wearing a face mask, the barista too. We could see only each other's eyes, skin creasing at our edges. The transaction was straightforward. I resented the wariness of each other that masks indicate.

I sat with my oat milk flat white and heard others' conversations, even if I didn't wish to, their voices in private exchanges carrying across the room to my perch at the window. My friend messaged me from Melbourne, telling me of the passing of her long-loved dog. Meanwhile she, along with everyone else there, is shut in. Locked down.

There have been words spoken around me and words offered to me as text; the air, my ears, and eyes, have been full of words.

Katie writes about listening for whimsy. My quietness today (though not only today) is attuning me to listening for whimsy, but I hear none this morning. I have not found whimsy within. I have not found it in the silence. I have not found it in what lies beyond words – the faint hum of traffic in the distance, my neighbor's miniature fountain from outside my open window, the stillness of the trees. Except for this, perhaps. Writing now, these words here. Not the words themselves, nor what lies behind or within them, but how the act of writing lifts towards and beyond the ordinary, connecting with its life that we so often miss. How it catches hold of something passing that we hadn't seen, and maybe didn't want to see, were resisting.

★★★

Whimsy is remembering what it is to be alive, to be in the body, in the world, in love, in place, in appreciation, in the political and enraged: it is a happiness that also holds the impossibility of happiness: it is not a happiness naïve to power, to injustice, to violence and oppression. We listen with whimsy for what's ignored, rendered invisible, silenced.

Looking Away to Look More Closely

Katie, Sunday August 16, 2020

We are back in lockdown in Auckland. This is the second lockdown; the first was interminable but somewhat novel. This second one feels harder, more unfair, more wearing. I want to hide under the covers, ignore the steady stream of email telling us what to do, asking me what to do, requiring me to do something. I don't want to move my class online, I don't want to think about all the implications. I have no choice about either of these things. The situation requires some kind of response. The situation requires multiple, urgent responses. In the midst of the urgent and constant email stream, I notice that calls for special issue papers keep popping up. The special issues all have COVID themes. I read the descriptors with disinterest, admiring those who seem to be able to pivot so quickly, to think through and write about what such a crisis might mean for their scholarship. But I feel a deep lethargy, I don't want to write about the virus and what it means, I don't want to think of this as an opportunity. Not yet.

So, now I go walking in the city, in my local neighborhood. One of my dogs is with me and people want to stop to pat him. I can tell they want to as they approach and then they remember – lockdown – and they pull away, step away, step aside. Sometimes they smile.

The shops are all closed, but the street is busier almost than usual. Despite it being winter, the sun is shining and the day is warm. People are out walking, out with kids, out with dogs, out on bikes. The city feels alive with moving creatures, alive with people and birds and dogs. Some cafés are selling takeaway coffee and food. People wait outside patiently in the sun, wearing masks, and I wonder how they will drink the coffee with the mask. What kind of negotiation they will have to do between coffee cup, mask, and dog lead. What kind of bargain between intimacy and distance. What kind of balance between fear and solitude and action. No one is sick. No one dares sneeze or sniff or shiver in public now.

Jonathan, February 2020

Back home from Malta, one Sunday I walk back along the long lower beach at North Berwick as it curves west to the edge of the town and harbor. I am slow, breathing deep, in the chill February air, gloved hands in pockets, head down in the wind. At least the sun is out. I step aside from the remains of a washed-up crab and reach the low stone wall of the tidal pool, close to the town. The narrow wall heads out to sea a few meters before it right-angles left, parallel to the beach, some distance before another left turn to complete the rectangle.

The tide is on its way in, the waves not yet beginning to lap into the pool. A minute and some twenty tentative paces later, I'm standing on the long far wall with my back to the still, numbing waters and looking out across the waves towards Bass Rock, a volcanic plug standing 100 feet high in the Firth of Forth. The Rock has been home to hermits and prisoners, has a well, battlements, and a chapel, and plays host to 150,000 northern gannets. Its gaol was notorious in the 17th century as the destination for political and religious prisoners such as the Scottish Covenanters.

Looking out at the rock, the water rising towards where I am standing, I am grateful for what I read now as the whimsy of those who built this pool last century. To contemplate a swim in the Scottish North Sea is out of place, perhaps, but in place at least as a call to walk its walls a few meters out to sea so a middle-aged man can imagine himself, for a moment, a streamlined, swooping gannet, at ease in its body.

Katie, January 2020

I go running along the path that has been built for bikes. It follows the coast line, overlooks the sea in places and dives into the tussock-covered dunes in others. It is hot on the path. As I run up a small hill, breathing hard, I come across a structure. It is made of driftwood and is a kind of chair with a wooden canopy. It overlooks the water, stares out to sea like a sentry. It holds a place, at once natural and seemingly of the dunes and the sea and the coast. But also, at once, clearly interventionist. An echo of peopled intervention. No, a collaboration between the beach and those who visit or perhaps live there. A monument to the intersection of the driftwood, the dunes and their outlook, the hands that collected and assembled a structure, the canvas of the ocean. And me, as I run and construct a kind of meaning from how the chair stares out to the sea, out towards Whakaari – the volcanic island in the distance that is visible from this beach; the scene of a tragedy only a few weeks back when her eruptions caused multiple deaths – who is blowing smoke into the air. The driftwood chair seems like a witness, marking the moment of the tragic, calling to the sea and the air and connecting me, as I run, to the dunes, the sky, the island, the deaths. It is a whimsical structure, evoking the earth's measured beat. A call for us all to witness and cohabitate. My body feels this as I run and I take it with me, through the days that follow and back now to my laptop and this writing. And this moment layers across and between the weeks – the deaths on Whakaari, my running, this writing and telling. I read the driftwood structure as whimsical – out of place but of the place at the same time – signaling to nothing in particular necessarily, and so, to something. It makes me think about how, sometimes, we can see things more clearly when we look at them indirectly. Looking away to look more closely, looking askance, like looking across the cold North Sea and being caught by the elegance and arcs of the sea-birds. Whimsy can be found that way, perhaps; we need to be open to it but not looking directly.

Jonathan, January 2020

In my work – writing as inquiry, creative-relational inquiry (e.g., Wyatt, 2019) – the notion of whimsy invites, permits, articulates, catches hold of, the possibility of surprise, the chance of being taken. I might be writing on a morning like this one at a gym, typing on my phone between sets, and something might happen. It might not, but it might. Perhaps; if I'm lucky; if I listen with whimsy, my thumbs on my ancient phone. Whimsical inquiry may be inquiry that stays open to not knowing, open to its imagination, just open, letting go. It's inquiry that resists the staid rationalism of the academy. Inquiry whose "ways of operating [are] more like those of an artist, rather than of [those] who are always haunted by an outmoded ideal of scientificity" (Guattari, 2000, p. 35).

There's a class every morning in the gym at this time. Today's is loud, with an incessant soundtrack and staccato shouts of encouragement. Out of sight behind the half-walls, the amplified voice wanting more seems incongruous, intrusive, the main body of the gym almost yogic. Here the music is gentle, the voices quiet, and the movements slow. There are about fifteen of us here amongst the free weights. A man and a woman training together, concentrating over deadlifts. A woman on her own at one of the racks, lifting a heavy bar overhead. A man with his personal trainer, just talking it would seem. Otherwise, it's what I take to be men, like me, training alone; each of us intent, focused, here for our own purposes. Bettering ourselves. Forgetting ourselves. Recovering ourselves. Engaged, each, in our own struggles or joys. Or something else, something less obvious, something outside clichéd narratives of men in gyms lifting weights. Something particular to each of us working with and against these stories we tell. Something not available to us, out of awareness.

> *Alone, I write to the beat of an unseen class*
> *and its calls for more*
> *I write amongst the dropping of weights,*
> *like muffled bells tolling with relief,*
> *and weighted balls flung to the floor,*
> *amongst the cheers and slapped hands,*
> *and the cries of success*

Alone, I rest, and write, eyes open, not looking,
breathing, and find not the striving, the strain, and the effort
but the tenderness of words written in held breaths
in the silk of muscle under skin
in how the body can hold its strength in the extension
and feel a poem for you – there –
as it lets go

Endings

In this chapter, we have attempted to show whimsy, as well as talk about whimsy. By writing our way into whimsy – listening for it in our writings and our experiences – we have looked indirectly at whimsy, suggesting that it is there, perhaps, in the background, in the body, in comparison and in-between. As a result, we have discovered in and through this writing that whimsy can be many things. It doesn't have to be overt like the yarn-bombing in Mann's (2015) article; it can be found in the juxtaposition of past and current writing, in the drive home from work, and in the banal everyday act of walking the dog with a mask on. We are struck by how there is whimsy in the temporal comparisons of our writings pre- and post-COVID-19. How effortless it was to travel and holiday and be at the beach not so long ago, before we adopted masks and distancing and new kinds of restriction. Whimsy can be found in the new ways we have had to negotiate intimacy and distance, connection, and solitude. Whimsy is there in the everyday. It can be expressed or sought in writing or can appear indirectly like someone inexplicably waving to a passing train, like writing a poem at the gym, like the graffiti on a railway carriage, or a driftwood sculpture on a remote beach. Whimsy reminds us of the relational and contextual, but it points there aesthetically and indirectly. Whimsy can be disruptive and powerful but it is a power that asserts itself gently, slowly, even arbitrarily. Nevertheless, it evokes emotion and can connect with desire, liveliness, discovery, and intensities of feeling.

Whimsy is identifiable in ethnographic writing practices, especially those that seek openness and uncertainty, and those that embrace getting lost. In this chapter, we have attempted to engage a "nonlinear, many-layered textuality" (Lather, 2007, p. 87) by working with temporality across prose as well as poetic forms of inquiry (Richardson, 2000, 2004). A little like poetry, whimsy does seem to assert itself in writing, experience, and research if we allow it, if we invite it. When we attend to the pause, there it is. Bauman (2002) argues that poets have a duty to uncover that which is there but hidden behind the walls of the obvious; the truths that might be underneath what we all believe to be true. "The poet" he argues "must refuse to serve up truths known beforehand and well-worn truths already 'obvious' because they have been brought to the surface and left floating there….those truths are not this 'something hidden' that the poet is called to uncover; they are, rather, parts of the wall that the poet's mission is to crush" (p. 359). We wonder if listening with whimsy allows us to see or hear beyond the accepted everyday meanings and accepted truths, to those that are present but which may be missed. Listening and writing with whimsy might help us to attend to the invisible in the everyday. The pause that we have gained from being locked down has enabled a break from the barrage of stress, pressure, and busyness. While the lockdowns all around the world have certainly created other stressors (loneliness, distance, fear, economic deprivation) there has also been relief. An excuse to stop. Traffic has halted in many cities and industrial noise and bustle have ceased. As the cities stopped, other things have become apparent. In Auckland, native birds came back in numbers into the city; people on bikes proliferated, and teddy bears appeared in the windows of houses as a game for children. Some days the pause gave us permission to turn off email, to walk away. The lockdown has created a pause where it's possible to look at the obscure, to notice the small, to notice the insignificant and the undemanding. To hear the birdsong, to connect in different ways. Whimsy is, perhaps, a kind of connection. Whimsy is an attention to the beautiful in the banal; an attention to the minutiae in the bustle of life.

References

Bauman, Z. (2002). Afterthought: On writing; On writing sociologically. *Cultural Studies <=> Critical Methodologies, 2*(3), 359–370.

Davies, B, Gottsche, M., & Bansel, P. (2006). The rise and fall of the neo-liberal university. *European Journal of Education, 41* (2), 305–319.

Denzin, N. (2015). Coda: The death of Data? In Norman K. Denzin & Michael D. Giardina (Eds.), *Qualitative inquiry and the politics of research* (pp. 197–206). CA: Left Coast Press.

Fitzpatrick, K. (2013). *Critical pedagogy, physical education and urban schooling.* New York: Peter Lang.

Guattari, F. (2000). *The three ecologies.* Translated by Ian Pindar and Paul Sutton. London: Athlone. Original edition, 1989.

Lather, P. (2007). *Getting lost: Feminist efforts toward a double(d) science.* Albany: State University of New York Press.

Mann, J. (2015). Towards a politics of whimsy: Yarn bombing in the city. *Area, 47* (1), 65–72.

Richardson, L. (2000). Writing: A method of inquiry. In N. K. Denzin & Y. S. Lincoln (Eds.), *Handbook of qualitative research* (2nd ed., pp. 923–948). London: Sage.

Richardson, L. (2004). Poetic representation. In J. Flood, S. Brice-Heath, & D. Lapp (Eds.), *Handbook of research on teaching literacy through the communicative and visual arts* (pp. 232–238). New York: Routledge.

Williams, R. F. G., & Doessel, D. P. (2018). *The economics of mental health care: Industry, government and community issues.* (Original publication 2001). London: Routledge.

Wyatt, J. (2019). *Therapy, stand-up, and the gesture of writing: Towards creative-relational inquiry.* London: Routledge.

SECTION III

Global Futures

7

STILL STUMBLING TOWARD INDIGENIZATION, RECONCILIATION, AND DECOLONIZATION: WE ACKNOWLEDGE THE LAND, NOW WHAT?

Patrick Lewis

In Canada, the Truth and Reconciliation Commission's (TRC) summary report came out in June 2015 with the final comprehensive report in December 2015. Within those reports are the 94 Calls to Action as delineated by the commission that will guide all Canadians in working toward reconciliation. The Liberal Government of Canada (Trudeau) in that same year committed to working toward all 94 Calls to Action. We are five years out on that work and it would seem by any measure we have not cut much of a trail on the way to reconciliation, nor indigenization and decolonization for that matter. So, what's a white settler to think, or rather do, to facilitate movement toward indigenization, reconciliation, and decolonization in the academy? It's actually not that difficult; one needs only act, but you *must* act, even sometimes transgressive acts; and it must be from a place of "relational accountability" (Wilson, 2009).

Since, and in some cases prior to, the TRC report, Canadian universities have been accelerating the movement to indigenize the academy as a form of reconciliation. Land or territorial acknowledgments started happening more often, and in more places so that now they are almost ubiquitous. These acknowledgments have been *and* are a very good first step, but there has not been much of a second step by many universities.

Let's be clear, the systems and structures of White settler society tend not to be answerable nor responsible to the discourses of decolonization and indigenization. But we as a community of scholars in the academy can be, *if we choose*. As for actually working toward decolonization, reconciliation, and indigenization in the academy there is a whole lot of heavy work to get after. So, what are some of the things that folks might do in their day-to-day practice within the academy to move further along the trail to reconciliation, indigenization, and decolonization? I think there is a responsibility on the part of the academy and in particular people in roles like my own (Associate Dean) to do the work to move toward reconciliation, indigenization, and decolonization.

Decolonization

First and foremost, we must recognize the legitimacy of Indigenous research and scholarship beyond the current moment. That is, faculties and departments must take up the work of reconciling Indigenous research and scholarship with current views and practices around settler research; of the peer review tenure and promotion process; and of course, the notion of equitable rather than equal workload. What does that look like? Well, it requires that universities create frameworks and policies that revise things like Annual Information Forms, provide resources to support Indigenous Scholars in their research work, and adjust workloads to ensure Indigenous scholars can thrive.

The academy tends to place significant demands upon Indigenous faculty members. Parallel with the usual expectations of all faculty, Indigenous faculty members are often expected to act as teachers and role models for non-Indigenous colleagues who are working toward reconciliation and indigenizing their own practices. While upholding standards of academic research and teaching which all scholars must meet, Indigenous faculty often face significant expectations from respective Indigenous communities outside the university where they are called to engage, serve, and share their expertise in collaborative and holistic ways. Establishing community connections and community building are time consuming yet integral to meeting the standards of responsible, ethical, and accountable Indigenous-centered research practices. Collectively, these commitments all have the potential to place an excessive and disproportionate burden on Indigenous faculty members who participate in Indigenous-centerd scholarship and research pedagogies (Faculty of Education, 2018).

However, it requires more than that, in that Indigenous research is invariable decolonizing work carried out in community(ies) for community, and universities need to acknowledge the importance of this work for those communities, but also recognize its value to the mission of universities which is to seek truth and advance understanding through research and teaching; it is about universities adapting to Indigenous research not the other way around. "Indigenous knowledge, then, represents an opportunity for the academy to expand the scope of what it now considers human understanding, and to include other knowledges made marginal by the myopic view of most contemporary scholarship" (Gaudry & Lorenz, 2018, p. 211).

Unfortunately, many colleagues who sit on university peer review committees are unfamiliar with Indigenous research and/or decolonization theory; I have been asked several times over the years to act as an external reviewer for

Indigenous colleagues at other universities who are applying for tenure or promotion because of my familiarity with Indigenous research and decolonizing theory. But we need many more colleagues in the academy and administrative positions to become familiar with this important work if we are being genuine with our assertions to indigenization and reconciliation. Decolonization is still perceived as relatively new in the academy; however, as Sium and Ritskes (2013) have noted "decolonization…has been practiced and engaged and theorized in Indigenous communities in ways that have already yielded rich, complex layers of thought" (p. ii). Indeed, Indigenous communities have been practicing and theorizing decolonization for almost 500 years through their ongoing resistance and struggle for survival from first contact with European settlers and their accompanying violent colonial structures and practices that, as Wolfe (1999 and 2006) notes was not an event in the past, but rather structural practices and institutions that have evolved (p. 163) and persists to this day. It is through the stories/storytelling of resistance and the resurgence of Indigeneity in these communities that we come to see that "…Indigenous epistemologies are disruptive, sustaining, knowledge producing, and theory-in-action. Stories are decolonization theory in its most natural form" (Sium & Ritskes, 2013, p. ii).

Decolonization is not new to Indigenous people across Turtle Island and around the world, it is an act of resistance and survival against the quotidian backdrop of colonial structures working to erode and erase indigeneity. It is important to recognize that Indigenous resistance is not just blockades or protests that gain media coverage. As Steinman (2020) reminds us, "Indigenous people resist the whole range of settler colonialism through a variety of actions" including memory activism with correcting histories, through language revitalization, renew traditional foods and practices, assert jurisdiction over Indigenous children and youth (p. 3), advocate for appropriate health care, and argue for the honoring of treaties nation to nation, to name only some of the forms of daily resistance. "We do not have to go looking for settler colonialism so that we can oppose it. We are in it, all the time, and we can act to undermine it where we are" (p. 4). Universities, and by consequence all of us in those institutions must see and acknowledge that Indigenous research "drags the vague notions of decolonization back to the immediate, relational, and spiritual underpinnings of Indigenous thought" (Sium & Ritskes, 2013, p. ii) and lived experience.

Even with the recent "turn to reconciliation" we are reminded that "Canadian universities have, for the majority of their existence, operated as a tool of de-indigenization, a legacy that now runs counter to many of the public statements on reconciliation found in institutional plans across Canada" (Gaudry & Lorenz, 2018, p. 221). Universities are centuries old colonial institutions in which the settler community has benefited from the most, and like all education institutions in Canada they have been utilized to work toward the assimilation and erasure of Indigeneity. There is enormous work needed to prise open a space for Indigenous epistemes, which numerous Indigenous scholars have been try-ing to do for many years (Alfred, 2004; Battiste, Bell, & Findlay, 2002; Deloria, 2004; Mihesuah & Wilson, 2004; Tuck & Yang, 2012; Wilson, 2009; to list only a few). As Rauna Kuokkanen (2008) has shown the academy has worked tirelessly to foster a "sanctioned epistemic ignorance" of Indigenous worldviews or any other views other than those drawn from the Western Enlightenment to create an academy that is at its foundation colonial. Such sanctioned ignorance is another example of Wolfe's (2006) assertion that colonization is not an event in the distant past, but an ever-present evolving structure. It is a structure that is already and everywhere "a form of subtle violence. When other than dominant epistemes and forms of knowing are not seen or recognized, they disappear" (Kuokkanen, 2008, p. 317).

Indigenization

Indigenization is an interesting term which has evolved to have multiple mean-ings and interpretation since it has entered the mainstream lexicon. However, we have to explore what is meant by the idea of indigenization; and what does it mean to universities, Indigenous scholars, Indigenous communities, and broader society? In general terms, indigenization requires a shift in thinking throughout current institutional and structural practices that allows for the introduction and integration of Indigenous knowledge systems. When this truly happens there will be a transformation in how we are in the world and our ethical relational-ity (decolonization). In the context of universities, this is perceived as bring-ing Indigenous knowledge systems together with Western knowledge systems. However, it must be noted that there is no single Indigenous knowledge sys-tem; each Indigenous Nation and/or community may have their own unique worldview. Certainly, there are similarities and commonalities across Nations, but it must be recognized that it is not a monolithic worldview. Consequently, when an organization like a university decides to indigenize there is an inher-ent responsibility to consult and work with the Indigenous community(ies) on whose land the university is located, first to acknowledge and recognize the validity of those Indigenous knowledges and perspectives, and then work to learn how those ways of knowing and being (worldview) can be integrated into the university.

Gaudry and Lorenz (2018) have analyzed and written about indigeniza-tion in the Canadian academy and found that there seems to be three mean-ings to indigenization that are not always compatible with each other. They show how the three meanings are on a spectrum calling them: indigenization inclusion—reconciliation indigenization—decolonial indigenization. Inclusion is the recruitment of more Indigenous students and staff while nothing much changes in the structures and practices of the institution and Indigenous students and Indigenous faculty have to learn to adapt to the university structures, practices, policies—quite simply white settler structures. Reconciliation indigenization situates Indigenous epistemologies and ontologies on the same footing as Canadian/Western knowledge systems and practices, accompanied by robust discussion of how the two may be reconciled and what relationship the university should have with Indigenous communities. And the third, decolonial indigenization aims for a complete deconstruction of the academy that creates something new with equitable power relations between Indigenous and non-Indigenous Canadians (pp. 218–219).

As mentioned above, many universities have embraced the notion of indigenizing the academy, but what that means seems to be fluid and open to interpretation by many post-secondary institutions. In 2018, Universities of Canada indicated that 70% of its member institutions have developed plans (or are in the process) for working toward reconciliation and indigenization. However, upon closer examination, I think we can see that we are currently in a period of "indigenization Lite", there is a lot of rhetoric recognizing past and current injustices and the need to reconcile and move forward in partnership, but what is actually happening is not exactly groundbreaking. What the majority of universities have been working on is recruitment into their institutions. It has been well documented that indigenization in the academy is decidedly on a path toward "Indigenous inclusion [which] is a policy that aims to increase the number of Indigenous students, faculty, and staff in the Canadian academy" (Gaudry & Lorenz, 2018, p. 218), all of which is good, but as mentioned that is hardly the extent of the idea of Indigenization.

The acceleration of Canadian universities indigenizing mentioned earlier has certainly slowed or rather has been tempered when faced with the actual transformational work that needs to be carried out by the institutions if something more than inclusion indigenization is to be realized. Consequently, there has been a shift to rhetorical language that "betrays that much of this 'reconciliation turn' has been more discursive than substantive, and that few policies that have aimed to uproot the established epistemological privilege of the Western tradition, remain a substantial minority" (Gaudry & Lornez 2018, p. 222). If we are sincere in the academy about indigenization it cannot be separated from decolonization if we are to move toward authentic reconciliation. It requires us all to become familiar with Indigenous ways of knowing and being and in that process come to respect and value those worldviews as equal to other views. Clearly, the academy has work to do just as the rest of broader Canadian society; decolonization and indigenization require the collaboration of Indigenous and non-Indigenous people, governments, organizations, and institutions. As Gaudry and Lorenz (2018) emphasize we have to work to "ensure that everyone understands that indigenization isn't just a 'pro forma' program, but rather a process built on collaboration, consensus, and meaningful partnership" (p. 225).

The Canadian Academy has embraced Indigenization, making plans, financial commitments, and policy. My own university (University of Regina) has created an office of Indigenization with an "Executive Lead", an Indigenous Advisory Circle to the President, the ta-tawâw Student Centre, Elders in Residence, and some attempts to revise programs and supports for Indigenous students. Our Faculty of Education has created a Chair of Indigenization and has an Elder in Residence and a Knowledge Keeper in Residence. However, more promising was that many universities were beginning to approach indigenization through having an Indigenous course requirement (ICR). In the early days of the release of the TRC there was great optimism that universities would use this approach across all degree programs; however, to date only the University of Winnipeg and Lakehead University have implemented that requirement (Gaudry & Lorenz, 2018, p. 222). But it has been mainly professional programs in Canadian universities (Education, Nursing, Social Work) that have implemented ICRs, some did so several years before the TRC report and Calls to Action were released (see Faculty of Education University of Regina). In these professional programs Indigenous content in their curricula has been well established as integral to students' professional development. Regardless of the abating enthusiasm for ICRs across university degree programs, "faculty who teach Indigenous studies, still overwhelmingly believe that ICRs have the potential to help settler Canadians gain greater understanding of Indigenous-Canada relations" (Gaudry & Lorenz, 2018, p. 222). This slow walk toward even requiring one ICR in each degree program stands in stark contrast to the statement from the Indigenous Advisory Circle at the University of Regina expressing that Indigenization is,

> the transformation of the existing academy by including Indigenous knowledges, voices, critiques, scholars, students and materials as well as the establishment of physical and epistemic spaces that facilitate the ethical stewardship of a plurality of Indigenous knowledges and practices so thoroughly as to constitute an essential element of the university. It is not limited to Indigenous people, but encompasses all students and faculty, for the benefit of our academic integrity and our social viability.
>
> (*Indigenous Advisory Circle, 2015, p. 7*)

Some universities, including the University of Regina, have done a lot of work, but "it does so largely by supporting the adaption of Indigenous people to the current (often alienating) culture of the Canadian academy" (Gaudry & Lorenz, 2018, p. 218). Administrators of most universities are unable or unwilling to actually enact some of their own rhetoric when it comes to indigenization because to embrace the notion of decolonial indigenization is perceived as too much of a paradigm shift, too disruptive, or too radical. Yet without university administrative support and financial commitments indigenization at many universities rides a precarious trail. Even with indigenization as inclusion the Indigenous student services and centers that many universities have created are often only short term funded and sometimes by external funders which make it challenging for the people working in these contexts (p. 221). We must also keep in mind that there is a need to build capacity with respect to Indigenous faculty and staff at many universities; the vast majority of faculty and staff are non-Indigenous. However, the academy must work to support and promote Indigenous faculty and staff if the institution is to actually move further along the Indigenization spectrum. Perhaps we need to think about indigenization as inclusion not as the "end goal… but rather as a strategy for building systemic indigenization of the Canadian academy" (p. 221). Universities in Canada have begun to cut a trail; however, we can see that there is much more work ahead of the academy if we are truly going to realize indigenization in a comprehensive, holistic, and authentic way.

Reconciliation

What is reconciliation in the Canadian context? In June 2015, after almost 7 years of work the Truth and Reconciliation Commission released their Executive Summary and the accompanying 94 Calls to Action with respect to reconciliation between Canadians and Indigenous peoples.

From the TRC it states that:

> Reconciliation is about establishing and maintaining a mutually respectful relationship between Aboriginal and non-Aboriginal peoples in this country. In order for that to happen, there has to be awareness of the past, an acknowledgement of the harm that has been inflicted, atonement for the causes, and action to change behaviour."
>
> *(TRC, 2015, p. 6)*

However, we must ask, What does that look like and how do we realize the aim of reconciliation? As we can see in the work of decolonization and indigenization, all of which are integral to reconciliation we have some work ahead of us. In order to fully appreciate the idea of reconciliation we have to consider what it really entails if we are serious about the work. We must understand that it is critical complex work that must be continuous and sustained and that it is a process not an event acknowledging the past injustices and harms, although that's part of it, but rather it is a process of healing and working toward inclusion and solidarity as a society and country. Reconciliation must be multifaceted as we work toward acknowledging and learning the history of Canada as a colonizing enterprise that worked to erase Indigenous people that still reverberate across generations with the legacy of residential schools and the Indian Act. It requires

Canada to acknowledge the treaties and honor them, respect Indigenous rights and titles, and the building of new relationships. It is the responsibility of every Canadian to engage with reconciliation to learn and welcome Indigenous worldviews and knowledges into Canadian society.

Reconciliation cannot easily be realized without the work of decolonization and indigenization if there is to ever be meaningful systemic change in the relationship between Indigenous people and non-Indigenous people of Canada. In the context of the academy reconciliation has been taken up rhetorically with the same alacrity of Indigenization, but again the work has been uneven, promising, and discouraging all at the same time. As mentioned, several universities have worked aggressively to recruit Indigenous faculty, staff, and students across multiple disciplines as well as Indigenous Studies. Noted earlier, many professional programs at several universities have worked very hard to integrate Indigenous knowledges and pedagogies into their programs through required courses, Elder-in Residence programs, and field experiences. However, universities need to remember that central to reconciliation is that it is a process of healing and repairing relationships between Indigenous and non-Indigenous people of Canada where trust has been broken for a very long time. Consequently, when a university begins to speak and make plans for indigenization as a means of reconciliation there must be a commitment on the part of the institution to work closely with the local Indigenous communities to develop and realize those plans if trust is ever to be rekindled.

However, in this time of reconciliation I think it's important to keep in mind the words of Billy Ray Belcourt:

> Reconciliation is an affective mess: it throws together and condenses histories of trauma and their shaky bodies and feelings into a neatly bordered desire; a desire to let go, to move on, to turn to the future with open arms, as it were. Reconciliation is stubbornly ambivalent in its potentiality, an object of desire that we're not entirely certain how to acquire or substantiate, but one that the state – reified through the bodies of politicians, Indigenous or otherwise – is telling us we need.
>
> (*Belcourt, 2016, p. 2*)

Reconciliation is a formidable task that can seem overwhelming in the face of trying to repair relationships that have been broken and dysfunctional for more than 150 years. It will not be easy and it will not happen quickly, in the words of Senator Murry Sinclair former chair of the TRC, "We have a lot of work to do, we're not just talking about changing a system. We're getting people to think differently" (Rubinstein, 2016). Universities have a central role in that work, if they choose to take it up in a sincere and genuine way. However, it requires long-term sustained commitment not just immediately but for generations;

universities must continue to implement their plans for reconciliation through indigenization so that eventually they move along that continuum toward decolonial indigenization and Indigenous knowledges and teachings are within the orbit of the university equally and equitably with Western knowledges and practices. It is imperative that universities recognize the enormity and complexity of reconciliation, but work collaboratively to realize the reparative process of reconciliation and commit to the sustained long-term aims of the Calls to Action.

Acknowledging the Land

In Canada, we are in a moment that whenever we are at a gathering of some kind it is rare not to hear an acknowledgment of the territory or the land upon which we are gathered. This has been a vitally important step, the first step in admitting the history of colonization and the removal of the land from Indigenous people and the removal of Indigenous people from their Land. But as stated at the outset—now what, where are the second, third, and fourth steps? We can see that it is uneven across the academic landscape of how universities are continuing to pursue indigenization. Sometimes there is promising commitment on the part of an institution, like that of the University of Saskatchewan, which not long after the TRC report had announced nationally through the media, plans, and resource commitments to increasing Indigenous Faculty and staff across disciplines in the Faculty of Arts and Science (Putnam, 2018). A university that already had established a significant number of Indigenous scholars in the College of Education and the associated Indian Teacher Education Program (ITEP). But in the summer of 2020 the University of Saskatchewan made headlines for the opposite reasons, with a byline of the exodus of Indigenous faculty and staff from the institution because of the "racism, a hostile work environment and the slow pace of reforms" (Warick, 2020). This is not to single out the University of Saskatchewan, but rather is demonstrative of how settler institutions that are purported to be on the vanguard of reconciliation through indigenization have an enormous amount of decolonizing work to do.

But, more importantly the racism experienced at the University of Saskatchewan removes the discussion of decolonization, indigenization, and reconciliation from the sometime rarefied halls of academia and reminds us of the stark reality of the lived experience of many Indigenous people prior to and 5 years after the TRC report and Calls to Action. There are still approximately 100 First Nations communities with boil water advisories; there is the ongoing chronic underfunding of First Nations K-12 Education and the legacy of residential schools contributing to lower levels of education completion; there is inadequate access to health care; significantly poorer health levels and a lack and/ or absence of mental health services; inadequate housing (44% of First Nation people live in dwellings that are in need of major repair); lower income levels with First Nations people earning only 75% of the income of non-Indigenous Canadians; First Nations people experience much higher rates of unemployment; the well documented higher rates of incarceration of Indigenous people who make up less than 3% of the Canadian population but represent 28% of admissions into custody; Indigenous children and youth have higher death rate from unintentional injuries; the ongoing issue of missing and murder Indigenous women and girls; the inordinately large number of Indigenous children and youth apprehended by social services; and the extraordinarily higher rates of suicide among Indigenous people, in particular youth.

Yes, there is indeed a great deal of work to be done not just at universities, but across all of Canadian society if there is to be any real movement toward reconciliation. Reconciliation is a responsibility of all Canadians, all our institutions, and all levels of government across all communities. As Murray Sinclair said, "we're getting people to think differently" (Rubinstein, 2016), which requires a significant shift within the Canadian psyche and we are still in the early days of that process because as Senator Sinclair said it will take generations. I began the chapter by saying we are stumbling toward indigenization, reconciliation, and decolonization and in many ways as I have suggested, that captures what has been happening since the release of the TRC report and Calls to Action. We need to do better, we can do better, and we must do better. But it requires more Canadians, in particular settlers to step up and do the groundwork, because "settlers can unsettle the interwoven beliefs, discourses and practices of our institutions and organizations" (Steinman, 2020, p. 15) to facilitate the process of decolonization, indigenization, and reconciliation. Universities and the K-12 educational system have key roles to play in that process and have begun to invest in that work and will have to continue to do so increasingly over the decades to come.

References

Alfred, T. (2004). Warrior scholarship: Seeing the university as a ground of contention. In D. Mihesuah, & A. Wilson (Eds.), *Indigenizing the academy: Transforming scholarship and empowering communities* (pp. 88–99). Lincoln, NE: University of Nebraska Press.

Battiste, M., Bell, L., & Findlay, L. M. (2002). Decolonizing education in Canadian universities: An interdisciplinary, international, indigenous research project. *Canadian Journal of Native Education, 26,* 82–95.

Belcourt, B.-R. (2016). Political depression in a time of reconciliation. *Active History.Ca: History Matters.* Retrieved from: http://activehistory.ca/2016/01/political-depression-in-a-time-of-reconciliation/

Deloria, V. (2004). Marginal and Submarginal. In D. Mihesuah & A. Wilson (Eds.), *Indigenizing the academy: Transforming scholarship and empowering communities* (pp. 16–30). Lincoln, NE: University of Nebraska Press.

Faculty of Education (2018). *Indigenous scholar recruitment and retention policy.* Regina, SK: University of Regina.

Gaudry, A. & Lorenz, D. (2018). Indigenization as inclusion, reconciliation, decolonization: navigating the different visions of indigenizing the academy. *AlterNative, 14*(3), 218–227.

Indigenous Advisory Circle (2015). *Indigenous Advisory Circle's definition of Indigenization in University of Regina Strategic Plan 2015–2020.* Regina, SK: University of Regina.

Kuokkanen, R. (2008). *Reshaping the university: Responsibility, indigenous epistemes, and the logic of the gift.* Vancouver, Canada: University of British Columbia Press.

Mihesuah, D. A., & Wilson, A. (Eds.). (2004). *Indigenizing the academy: Transforming scholarship and empowering communities.* Lincoln, NE: University of Nebraska Press.

Putnam, C. (2018). *College Unveils Aboriginal Faculty Recruitment Plan.* Retrieved from: https://artsandscience.usask.ca/news/articles/1791/College_unveils_Aboriginal_faculty_recruitment_plan

Rubinstein, D. (2016). *From Truth to Reconciliation: Murray Sinclair at Carleton.* Retrieved from: https://newsroom.carleton.ca/story/truth-and-reconciliation-commission/

Sium, A., & Ritskes, E. (2013). Speaking truth to power: Indigenous storytelling as an act of living resistance. *Decolonization: Indigeneity, Education & Society,* (2)1, i–x.

Steinman, E. (2020): Unsettling as agency: Unsettling settler colonialism where you are, *Settler Colonial Studies.* DOI: 10.1080/2201473X.2020.1807877.

TRC (2015). *Honouring the Truth, Reconciling for the Future Summary of the Final Report of the Truth and Reconciliation Commission of Canada.* Retrieved from: www.trc.ca

Tuck, E., & Yang, W. K. (2012). Decolonization is not a metaphor. *Decolonization: Indigeneity, Education & Society, 1*(1), 1–40.

Universities Canada (2018). Retrieved from: https://www.univcan.ca/priorities/indigenous-education/

Warick, J. (2020). Indigenous professors cite racism, lack of reform in University of Saskatchewan exodus. *CBC News.* Retrieved from: https://www.cbc.ca/news/canada/saskatoon/indigenous-professors-cite-racism-lack-of-reform-in-university-of-saskatchewan-exodus-1.5703554

Wilson, S. (2009). *Research is ceremony: Indigenous research methods.* Winnipeg, MB: Fernwood Publishing.

Wolfe, P. (1999). *Settler Colonialism.* New York, NY: Cassell.

Wolfe, P. (2006). Settler colonialism and the elimination of the native, *Journal of Genocide Research, 8*(4), 387–409. DOI: 10.1080/14623520601056240.

8

SLOW-MOTION ACTIVISM: PERFORMING IMPOSSIBLE FUTURES

Magdalena Kazubowski-Houston

Performances of the Impossible

My interlocutor, Randia, an elderly Romani woman, and I are developing a dramatic script based on her life. More than a recitation of lines, this involves full-fledged acting in which Randia and I assume the roles of different characters. Randia plays the protagonist, Córka, also an elderly Romani woman, who is telling the audience (me) about her daughter's terminal illness. From such dramatic storytelling sessions, I learn about Randia's life in Poland after her children moved abroad. I have been conducting this ethnographic dramatic storytelling project with Randia for several years now, and she usually develops her scenes through spontaneous improvisations with little or no preparation or prior discussion. This year, however, although still excited to perform, Randia has begun taking more time to develop her scenes and working a lot slower.

After Poland's accession to the European Union, in 2004, many young and middle-aged adults have migrated to other countries; my project uses dramatic storytelling to understand how these migrations have impacted the lives of their Romani elders. Many have been fending for themselves since Poland joined the European Union, which opened access to Western labor markets, and the 2007 Schengen Treaty, which eliminated tourist visa requirements for Polish citizens (White 2011). Romani elders are some of those most affected by these migrations (Kazubowski-Houston 2012) and by other socioeconomic transformations that have deteriorated Romani minorities' quality of life. Negative stereotypes, combined with economic crises and resurgent Polish nationalism have increased acts of prejudice, marginalization, and violence against the Roma (Jasinska-Kania 2009). Consequently, nearly 60 percent – and in some regions up to 90 percent – of Poland's Roma have migrated to Western Europe. Many of the Roma I have worked with report that some Romani communities in Poland are now populated primarily by the elderly, often widows, who are unable to travel abroad due to their advanced age and/or ill health (Kazubowski-Houston 2012; see also the work done by *Zwiazek Romow Polskich* [Polish Roma Union]). The mid-sized city of Elbląg in northern Poland where I conducted my research has one of the country's oldest populations, an unemployment rate of approximately 20 percent (between 2010 and 2015) (Powiatowy Urząd Pracy w Elblągu), and high migration rates among Romani (Kazubowski-Houston 2012). Nearly all of Randia's children and grandchildren have left Poland in search of employment. Randia's pension is meager and she lives in a decrepit government-subsidized apartment block. Suffering from heart disease, diabetes, high blood pressure, and, most recently, blindness, Randia finds living alone increasingly arduous.

Today, Randia, as Córka, begins improvising a scene by standing tall and radiant, energetically gesticulating, and walking back and forth. Córka tells the audience (me) that her daughter, Hania, was diagnosed with metastatic lung cancer while living abroad. Once her illness had significantly progressed, she returned to Poland to be cared for by Córka, as Hania's husband, who worked long hours at a gas station, was unable to provide the round-the-clock care she needed. When Hania arrived in Poland, the doctors gave her only a few weeks to live. Weak, emaciated, and losing hair from chemotherapy, she spent her days in bed, in and out of consciousness. Córka lowers her voice and explains that she cared for Hania day and night, caressing her hair, wiping her forehead, feeding her spoonfuls of chicken soup, and moistening her lips. Then she turns her back to the audience, and slowly, precisely traces an outline of a human figure in the empty space ahead of her, above eye level. Then she repeatedly performs –nearly in slow motion – her actions of caring for Hania, with outmost gentleness, kindness, and attention. She summons her son and uncle to help her turn Hania over so she can rub her back with alcohol because, she notes, this is what has saved Hania from getting bedsores. Next, she pauses and listens to Hania intently. After a few seconds, she turns around and tells the audience that, one night, Hania's condition deteriorated. She was taken to a hospital to die there. Córka and her entire family were devastated. Praying all night, Córka awaited the fateful call from the hospital, but the call never came. Hania did not die. The door swung wide open and Hania walked in, all fashionable and vigorous, her hair thick and beautiful, bouncing from side to side. Hania had been given an additional round of chemotherapy and recovered. 'Because', Córka concluded, 'things can happen that way, can't they? … The impossible can happen!'

But the impossible did not happen for Randia. Her daughter, Zefiryna, who lived in England, also had lung cancer and, like Hania, decided to return to Poland so her mother could care for her. However, unlike for Hania, there was nothing that doctors could do for Zefiryna. Her cancer was too advanced, as she had ignored symptoms for months and continued working long shifts in a meat-processing factory. She died a couple of weeks later. When Randia finished performing as Córka, I asked: 'Is this how you wish things were for you?' She replied, 'No, this could have never happened to me. [...] It could only happen to Córka – only Córka could undo death'.

Performance Ethnography and Activism

In this chapter, I want to rethink the activist potential of performance ethnography, a cross-disciplinary research approach that employs theatre and performance as a form of ethnographic process and/or representation (Conquergood 1988; Culhane 2011; Denzin 2003; Fabian 1990; Irving 2011; Kazubowski-Houston 2010, 2011, 2017; Madison 2010; Magnat 2011; Schechner 1985; Turner & Turner 1982). The collaborative, embodied, affective, and imaginative means of expression within performance have been seen as particularly conducive to engaging wide and diverse audiences. Some argue that an 'experiential and participatory methodology' (Conquergood 1998, 31) can 'put culture into motion' (Rosaldo 1989, 91) and facilitate a process of knowledge construction that 'speaks to and with' – not 'about and for' – the other[1] (Conquergood 1985, 10). Such knowledge construction takes place not only at a discursive level but also through embodiment and affect, and, thus, can potentially engage participants and audiences in more tangible and empathic ways (Conquergood 2002; Kazubowski-Houston 2017, 2018).

Most performance ethnography approaches, however, have conceptualized activism if not as a grandiose, vocal, and highly visible action, then at least 'as a standpoint or self-aware commitment' (Horton and Kraftl 2009, 17). Performance ethnographers hailing from anthropology have been largely invested in the discipline's recent efforts to reimagine itself as an engaged, collaborative, reflexive, and interventionist practice (Clarke 2010; Hemment 2007; Johnston 2010; Kline and Newcomb 2013; Osterweil 2013; Salazar et al. 2017). In the fields such as theatre and performance studies, performance ethnographers have drawn on the Brechtian[2] idea of politicization as social critique and/or transformative political action, and on its later iterations, including the notions of 'radical performances' ('acts that question or re-envision ingrained social arrangements of power' [Cohen-Cruz, 1998, 1]) and 'performance[s] of possibilities' (Madison, 2005, 172) that lead toward change. Most recent performance ethnography approaches have examined imagination as a space between the self and not-self (Sime 2007, 48) that can open up possibilities for different experiences and imaginaries and, as such, constitute a ground for action (Appadurai 1996, 7). However, even these imaginative approaches conceptualize intervention largely in strategic and goal-oriented terms (Elliott & Culhane 2016; Kazubowski-Houston 2017; Kazubowski-Houston & Magnat 2018; Salazar et al. 2017; Sjöberg 2017, 2018).

In contrast, I focus in this chapter on how performance employed as ethnography can facilitate an activism that works slowly and subtly, creating embodied and affective imaginaries with inadvertent transformative capacities. I trace how, in my dramatic storytelling project, such activist imaginaries have been staged as performances of impossible futures, bringing together reality, fiction, and human and spirit worlds. In particular, I discuss how the project's 'untidy creativity' (Gilchrist 2000, 2009) constituted a politics of intimacy (Pain and Staeheli 2014) through the magical labor of grief. As such, this chapter contributes to ongoing transdisciplinary debates on the activist potential of performance ethnography and offers a performance-based lens on the scholarship that theorizes the nature of contemporary politics that are enacted through 'gently subversive, interpersonal, or creative acts' (Pottinger 2017, 215).

The Magical Labor of Grief

'The impossible could only happen to Córka', asserts Randia, as 'only Córka could undo death'. It could never happen to her, Randia. Yet, Córka is only a character in the play, while Randia is a real person, grieving. What can we make of Randia's assertion? What if we take it to mean, for example, the direct opposite of what it seems to imply: Randia did actually hope for the impossible to happen to her and, in fact, did try to undo her daughter's death. Anthropologist Clifford Geertz (1973, 45) once famously argued that 'one of the most significant facts about us is that we all begin with the natural equipment to live a thousand kinds of life but end up in the end having only lived one'. We, as human beings, Geertz suggests, have an indefinite potential to live many different lives, but this potential is curtailed by our specific sociocultural conditioning. Extending Geertz's argument, anthropologist Andrew Irving (2018, 390) posits that our being in the world is defined by the negotiation of contingency and necessity. Contingency is linked to one's body, birthplace, nationality, ethnicity, gender, and economic status, as well as chance and luck; necessity, on the other hand, can be understood as how these contingencies unfold in contexts of global politics, fate, and law. I argue that our dramatic storytelling sessions have allowed Randia to temporarily circumvent both the contingency and necessity of her own life, and to live a different life in which she was able to undo her daughter's death. And I do mean 'live', not 'pretend' or 'act' or 'imagine'. Once Randia mused, 'If only one could choose to live a different life, just like that, wouldn't that be nice? If you could just switch... Don't like your life? Take someone else's. [Laughs.] But you know, yesterday, I was living Córka's life... I *really was*'. I pressed her: 'You mean, like, you totally became her? Like your life and hers merged together?' 'No', she insisted, 'I'm a different person, and she is a different [person] [...] My life has nothing to do with Córka's... but, for that moment, I lived her life'.

Clearly, Randia's attempts at undoing death were performances of the impossible; in real life, it had not been possible to save her daughter. Randia's scenes can be understood as stagings of what American author Joan Didion, in her memoir *The Year of Magical Thinking*, has called 'magical thinking'. Influenced by anthropological theorizing on magic as a belief in the cosmic interconnectedness of things, Didion (2005) defines magical thinking as a thought process by which she sought to come to terms with the death of her husband. She recounts the year spent, following her husband's death, looking for signs in her everyday life – omens in the form of, for example, undeleted emails and spelling mistakes – indicating that he would eventually return. Didion describes her magical thinking as a powerful way of denying reality, a way of keeping the deceased alive, despite all logic, and a way of filling the space of absence.

Randia's undoing of death could also be seen as a form of magical thinking, but unlike for Didion, it was not a way of denying that her daughter had died. On the contrary, Randia seemed to have firmly rooted herself in the impossibility of changing her own life, while also improvising a different possibility in a life that ultimately did not belong to her. This may have been the case because within the liminal, subjunctive ('as if') space of performance – between reality and fiction – magical thinking does not need deny reality but can simply propose an alternative one. Brian Massumi (2002, 134) writes about a 'thinking feeling' that unites thought and sensation, and performance's ability to construct ethnographic knowledge through such thinking feeling also may have contributed to this labor of magic. While improvising, Randia was able to tap into her affective interiorities, her unarticulated and subliminal bodily sensations, moods, wishes, and thoughts (Irving 2011; Massumi 2002). Doing so allowed her to conjure up new ways of being, dreams, and desires, which shifted focus toward what might surface, sprout, and promise (Crapanzano 2004; Kazubowski-Houston 2017; Mittermaier 2011).

According to Mikhail Bakhtin (1986, 126), our interior dialogues often have various 'superaddressees', ranging from people we know personally to those we do not, and even imaginary and fictional personas. In a context of performance, the interior dialogues of magical thinking can be staged in symbolic, metaphoric, and fictional forms through characters, performers, audience members, or offstage personas, to which performers can direct their thoughts and feelings (Irving 2018; Kazubowski-Houston 2017a, 2017b, 2018; Kazubowski-Houston and Magnat 2018; Salazar et al. 2017). It seems that in the dramatic storytelling sessions, Randia's staged her magical thinking as the dramatis personae of Córka and Hania, and their alternative reality in which Hania does not die. Randia's unique style of acting, which cannot be easily categorized in terms of Western approaches to performance, also seemed to have aided her efforts to undo death. Rather than seeking to convey an emotional identification with the character (in the Stanislavskian sense),[3] or to present the character in a detached, Brechtian manner or in a magic realist fashion that fused realistic and fantastical elements, Randia always insisted that she *was* the character. She inhabited Córka's life; her own life was not merged into that of her character, but was merely an anchor, a point of return, from which she ventured out.

Grief certainly was a major driving force in Randia's stagings of her magical thinking. The meticulous slow-motion gestures of caring for Hania that Randia had enacted as Córka may have been ways of expressing grief. In popular literature, blogs, and grief support websites, people stricken by grief frequently describe their experiences as living in slow motion, in a bubble where time stands still, while outside the world continues on.[4] Randia herself once told me that when the undertakers came to take Zefiryna's body away, she saw them walk in through the door and cover her daughter in a white sheet, while her son signed forms, and that it felt like she was not part of what was going on, merely observing her living room from a distance. That grief was a driving force behind her performances of the impossible was evident in her multiple admissions of feeling guilt over Zefiryna's death, as in the following conversation I had with her one day when we were on a break from storytelling:

> So, I was sitting by Zefiryna… as she laid right here in the living room. We rented a special bed from the hospital to make her comfortable. She was so thin and needed a comfortable bed, so that's… I wouldn't have her lying on an iffy bed! And I was sitting there beside her… [I] was getting tired because I didn't sleep all night… many nights… and she was breathing hard, and, for a minute, I thought, 'What was that?' But then she wasn't making any sounds, so I thought she may've been snoring. She has a nose – maybe a cold – her breathing was loud. And then I fell asleep and I heard her breathing loudly again. And then I thought to myself, when Włodek [her son] returns, then I'll ask him to check on her. I'm blind, so couldn't check myself. And I thought she was fine, but she wasn't… she was dying. My child was dying… right there, in front of me. Maybe… maybe had I called a doctor, she would've lived? I mean, no, she wouldn't… there's no way she'd survive, but maybe… I don't what I'm saying.

On another occasions, Randia admitted, 'You know, Magda, sometimes I have such a feeling… such guilt… that maybe I could have saved [Zefiryna], but I had nothing more to sell and no one to help. Also, how could I've done anything, when I can't see? I'm not like Córka… she had money… she was from a wealthier family… there are Romani women who are better off, you know?'

Randia' attempts to undo death may have helped her to work through some of the guilt, disbelief, anger, confusion, and profound sadness that she had felt since her daughter's passing. Some time after performing the scene in which Hania does not die, Randia confided in me that Zefiryna's nightly visitations 'felt different'. Although Zefiryna was still visiting frequently, she seemed, to Randia, 'somehow more distant, peaceful… as if she [were] merely passing by'. However, this does not mean that the dramatic storytelling necessarily alleviated Randia's guilt. In fact, to a certain extent, it may have added an additional level of culpability. Randia once expressed a concern that, in performing a scene in which Córka's daughter does not die, she may have 'somehow disrespected Zefiryna'. As well, she worried that Zefiryna may have felt betrayed that her mother performed a scene in which her character manages to save her daughter's life. She wondered, 'Why am I [as Córka] saving someone else's child and not my own?'

Still, as far as Randia's grief was concerned, perhaps the dramatic storytelling did something else. Death and bereavement have a tremendous impact on people's lives because they force us to live with absence. According to Avril Maddrell (2018, 505), rather than provoking an awareness of their absence, the dead continue to be emotionally present for the living. Grief works through the maintaining of emotional bonds with the dead through cemeteries, memorials, shrines, photographs, commemorative objects, and affective rituals and performances (Maddrell 2018, 507). Perhaps Randia's dramatic storytelling enabled her to maintain emotional bonds with her daughter by undoing death. Perhaps this is why, with time, Randia found that Zefiryna's nightly visitations 'felt different'.

Slow-Motion Activism

Reflections from an Unfolding Fan

Randia's performances of the impossible, however, cannot be seen as merely grief-stricken escapes into magical thought or the working through of grief. I argue that they were what I call 'slow-motion activism' that inspired critical reflection and built new worlds premised on reciprocal care at the intersection of reality, fiction, and human and spirit worlds. The dramatic storytelling sessions seemed to create a space where Randia was able to reflect on and critically evaluate her own life. She noted, for example, in an implicit contrast with her own life, that Córka was able to save her daughter because she was 'younger, healthier, and was able to hire best doctors', and because Hania had a caring, loving husband. In the following observation she remarked that Córka was able to 'care for her daughter properly' and 'act […] on time' because:

> she had her family around… someone was always there looking out for her. You know, because she had money and came from a rich family, her children were able to visit often. They also cared – came just to spend time with her, to help her out. They'd even send her money. The lives that some

people have! My God… I can't imagine. My kids sending me money?! I can't even imagine that… It is simply impossible. They barely have money to survive there.

Randia frequently interrupted her performances as Córka to speak of the difficulties she had encountered while caring for Zefiryna. She stressed that her progressing blindness was her biggest obstacle. When Zefiryna arrived at her house, gravely ill, Randia had already lost most of her sight and, living, on the upper floor of a building with no elevators, was basically confined to her apartment. Randia had come of age in the communist Poland of the 1950s and 1960s, when people – if they were lucky, given the extensive housing shortages – were allocated apartments in state-owned enterprises (SOEs) or cooperatives (Markham 2013). Such so-called *bloki*, constructed from concrete panels, usually had four or five levels but no elevators. Given this inaccessibility of socialist infrastructure, many members of Randia's generation, now in their seventies or older, find themselves prisoners in their own homes. Randia told me that caring for her dying daughter was difficult because she could not easily do her own shopping or take Hania to medical appointments. Her neighbors did provide some assistance, and one of her sons had come from England to help for a short while. Only when her younger son, Włodek, was released from prison did she finally receive more help. But even with Włodek around, she was still responsible for bathing and feeding her daughter, and for keeping vigil day and night.

One sunny afternoon, when Randia and I were sitting and eating cake in her living room, she remarked:

> When I think of Córka's life…well, she didn't have it easy, by any means, as a Gypsy woman, she didn't have it – but had more, how do you put it? – just, I guess, more luck in life. With her family, and children, and just… sometimes, I wonder, what my life would've looked like if I were born a different woman. A Polish woman… a German woman… or an English woman? If I were schooled like you are? Would I raise my children differently? Would the dead ones… would my dead children still be alive? Maybe I did things wrong? I'm a simple woman… But then, I think, no, I did everything right… I did everything right that a woman like me could do. Because what else could I have done? You're born who you are, and you live a life that's given to you… and you do your best. As a poor Gypsy woman, I think I did everything…

She reached a similar conclusion, that she had little means to help her ill son:

> You know, I was thinking yesterday after we finished recording [the dramatic storytelling sessions], that if – So, I was going to put aside some

money, little by little... My son is very ill too, so I thought, 'well, maybe I could at least help him one day'. But, now, when I think about it... what could I really do? Put away a zloty per day? When I don't really even have that? I can't really put away something I don't have. All my life I tried really hard, but now it's enough. My own end is near, anyway. I can't do more than I can. One day, I might lose him too...

What seems apparent from these excerpts is that Randia used the dramatic storytelling sessions to reflect on the contingencies of her life, her daughter's, and her family's, especially those linked to gender, ethnicity, and economic status.

Such reflections were further aided by Randia's scene-development process, choreography, and the ontology of her performance as reflected in her unique acting style. Randia's process of scene creation can be metaphorically visualized as the unfolding of a handheld fan, where each of its folds depicts a different life, each revolving on a pivot of Randia's life. Take, for example, how Randia went about developing the scene between Córka and Hania. She performed a few versions of this scene over a period of two weeks. In the first version, Córka's daughter, Hania, does not survive. One night, Hania's condition deteriorates, and she begins breathing heavily. While Córka hears strange sounds coming from Hania, she fails to identify them as death's rattle, the sounds of terminal respiratory secretions made by a person nearing death. Being blind, she is unable to clearly assess her daughter's state of health. Hania passes away under Córka's watch, but it is not until Hania's brother, Wojtek, arrives and calls an ambulance that Córka realizes what has happened. Randia performed two slightly different versions of this scene – one in which Hania passes away at home, and the other in which she survives for a few days in a hospital – before improvising the one in which Hania does not die. When I asked Randia why she had decided that Hania should not die, she remarked, 'When I was [acting], I felt such emptiness. So I decided that Córka's daughter should live. I couldn't do it to her'. From that feeling of impossible emptiness that Randia ventured out to live a different life and undo her daughter's death.

The first iteration of the scene corresponded closely to Randia's life. Randia cared for Zefiryna for two weeks, but when, one day, Zefiryna's breathing had altered, Randia missed this as a sign of dying and neglected to call paramedics. Randia's son found Zefiryna without vital signs, and a doctor confirmed her death minutes later. The overlap between the version of the scene in which Hania dies and the events of Randia's life is also made apparent in the fact that Randia made Córka blind, like herself. In contrast, in the scene in which Hania survives, Córka is not blind, and Randia had frequently used this scene to contrast it with her own life. The overlap between Córka's and Randia's lives in this scene was also evident when, Randia – through a slip of the tongue – referred to

Hania as Zefiryna. Randia recognized that the scene in which Hania dies corresponded closely to her own life, but she still maintained her unique ontology of performance, arguing that her life and Córka's were two separate lives: 'My life is my life, I live my life as me, separate from my characters. But when I'm Córka, then I'm totally her'.

This ontology of performance was also, to a certain extent, reflected in the choreography that Randia created, especially when, as Córka, she turned around and performed her actions of caring for Hania in an empty space, tracing Hania's body in the air above eye level, clearly separating that space from the space that she and I occupied. But when I asked her about this use of space, she replied that she was not aware of what she had done; the choice appeared to be unintentional. Notwithstanding, Randia's choreography is telling metaphorically. As she was undoing her daughter's death in another life, it may have been fitting to physically place the performance's action on a different spatial level. And, by adopting a slow-motion choreography, which symbolically stretches and slows down time on stage, Randia also seemed to have placed the performance's action in a temporality distinct from her own.

Perhaps for Randia, even within the liminal and fictional space of performance, the only way to 'really' live an impossible life in which her daughter does not die, was to travel back in time. When I asked Randia why she had slowed down her movements as Córka when she was caring for Hania, she explained:

> Córka has to do everything right. Slowly, no rush, when caring for a gravely ill person there should be no rush. And [Hania] came back home earlier, so she [Córka] has plenty of time to care for her. Maybe Zefiryna – maybe I didn't [do] enough – maybe I could? … more? [pauses, thinking]. But she's gone now. The clock can't be turned back. If she [Zefiryna] lived here, I could have taken care of her properly, maybe she would've survived? Who knows? She wanted to go to *that* [with emphasis] England… Why did she go? If I knew things would've turned out that way, I would've never let her go. Then she really wanted to return… she felt she was very ill, but she couldn't afford it. Her husband wouldn't give her money, so when she finally returned, it was too late [...] If she had lived, I would've gotten her to see doctors sooner. But Córka… she can care for Hania now. There is time. She can enjoy the care. It's a pleasure to care for one's child. There is no rush… Time is your enemy – if she rushes, the time will come when her daughter is gone.

> MAGDA: But Córka's daughter doesn't die?
> RANDIA: No, she doesn't, but Córka doesn't know that yet. When she cares for her daughter, she doesn't… Her daughter could die, like mine did. That's why she cherishes those moments with Hania. Hania had

returned before it was too late, as she had the means. A caring husband, and a healthier, younger mother. I was so ill already, and blind. It was very hard. The entire two weeks [after Zefiryna returned to Poland] I was rushing – it was like in a windmill – to do everything, to save her. I'd like to go back, now, and do it properly. Get better doctors… I don't know. Even if she were to die though, because, who knows, perhaps nothing could have saved her? But to caress my daughter's hair, hold her hand, and even feel her spirit leave her [body]. Because, because, I can't remember, I can't remember most, I can't… any of it. All went so fast, and then she was gone. If I could just hold onto that, that moment before she died. One last time…

While Randia explained that she had adopted the slow-motion movements because she wanted Córka to do 'everything right' in caring for her daughter, I also know that she was familiar with slow motion as a theatrical stylization technique. Her favorite TV series used slow motion to portray memory flashbacks and, on several occasions, Randia commented that she enjoyed watching 'those moments from the past'. Moreover, Randia would have been acquainted with a slow-motion technique from her participation in my performance ethnography project a decade earlier (Kazubowski-Houston 2010), when she had choreographed a flashback of a wedding scene in slow motion. And while she did not intentionally use slow-motion choreography in her scene between Córka and Hania, it may have offered – on an unconscious level – a perfect performative means of going back to the past and holding onto 'that moment before [Zefiryna] had died'.

This process of scene development, which revealed different lives in a fan-like fashion, combined with Randia's distinctive acting style that allowed her to live Córka's life as a distinct reality while simultaneously being firmly grounded in her own, and with the choreography that placed the lives of Randia's characters in a time and space distinct from her own, may have enabled Randia to observe, experience, feel, and reflect on the similarities and differences between the various lives. Also, slow-motion action on stage possesses a defamiliarizing potential, in the Brechtian sense, that can, by making the familiar strange, inspire critical reflection.

Feeding the Dead

Randia's performances of the impossible did more than simply inspire her to reflect on the contingencies of her own life. They were also activist practices of futuremaking that strove to build important relations of reciprocal care. Córka's slow-motion gestures of caring for Hania may also have constituted meticulous, stubborn, and intimate efforts of reconstructing, albeit inadvertently, the family and community that Randia had lost due to migration, illness, death, poverty, and racism. This is how Randia once spoke about her losses:

> When all my children left me, I'm here alone. All my people are gone. I try to live and do everything I did always, but it's like I'm left all alone in this world. Because, Magda, who am I without my people? How am supposed to live? But also, you know, how to die? Who will care for me, tend to me when I'm ill? I cared for my mother, but who will for me? Who will bury me? I'm asking now, 'Who will bury me?' I buried my children already, three of them. They're not coming back. And what if my living children can't come [to bury me]? We, Romani people, bury in our own way; not like you Poles; we do things differently… You know, I also – I liked my family around. I would always cook dinner. Every day I'd make a big pot of soup, and then a second dish, depending, sometimes meat, sometimes a hen, or even pancakes… those good Gypsy pancakes… I really cared for my family. I cared very well. These are my duties as a mother and grand-mother. This made – like I felt alive, but now I just barely cook twice per week. I'll make myself a pot of soup and eat it all week, and sometimes I don't even feel like making anything. Why would I? How do I do all that now? I haven't really figured that out.

Perhaps Randia's performances of the impossible constituted her way of 'figur[ing] out' how to live a life without those 'duties as a mother and grand-mother' that made her feel 'alive'. One day, she remarked, 'When we are record-ing [the play], I try – it's as if I'm speaking to my children. And I can hear them. I even know what they'd answer! [laughs]. It's like a chance to… I don't know what that is'. The dramatic storytelling sessions may have provided a chance for Randia to care for and be cared for by those she had lost. In the face of the preju-dice, discrimination, and deterritorialization that have ruptured familiar social networks, relationships, and cultural practices among the Roma, maintaining active kinship relations and community bonds has always been paramount among those with whom I have worked. Activism can be enacted through community-making practices, a means of counteracting adversity in which community can symbolically stand for 'protection and wellbeing' (Hackney et al. 2016, 36).

Randia's attempts to rebuild her communal networks were also evident in a scene that she created in which Córka tells her cousin, Agnieszka, that she needs to prepare a meal before she retires for bed. In the following excerpt, Randia switches roles between Córka and Agnieszka.

CÓRKA: Okay, Agnieszka, you can sit here. Help yourself – guest home, God home. Eat and drink… Whatever we've got, you're welcome to it! But now I have to make dinner.

AGNIESZKA: Cooking so late? You can make a fresh dinner tomorrow.

CÓRKA: I need a fresh dinner tonight. It's for Bożena. You never know… She died hungry, so….

AGNIESZKA: What does she want from you? Is she bothering you? Aren't you afraid?

CÓRKA: Why would I be afraid of my own child? She comes for food. She was hungry when she died, so she's looking through the cupboards, and sometimes the fridge. I know she'd like a warm meal, a warm meal in an empty stomach is good. I'll make her chicken soup and leave it here. She'll eat with such taste! She used to love my chicken soup. She's calling out to me, you know. So, I tell her, you know, I talk to her sometimes, that I'm here. I say, 'Come here, child, tell me what you want. I'll give you everything. I will help you. How can I help you?' You know, my mother, when she died – my God, I miss her so – she called out to me, too. She was unhappy, she would come and just stand there, breathing heavily. *That* [with emphasis] would frighten me! So, you know, my mother had asthma and she suffered a lot. And, then, when I requested a mass intention, she calmed down. She stopped coming. Now, my child's calling me. I have to tend to her. This is my child, so I have to. She was everything to do me and she called out to me. One has to care for the dead just like one cares for the living.

AGNIESZKA: Your daughter comes because she knows you'd do anything for her, you were such a great mother. Your kids don't appreciate it… You were too good.

CÓRKA: But my daughter is with me… She was a good child. She always came over and helped me with cleaning and errands. Just too bad she drank. It was that husband of hers. If she didn't [drink], she'd still be alive. I miss her so much. But she's with me… every day, making sure that I'm managing… You know, when my son died, I was so broken. He was my favourite. I haven't seen him for a long time. When his wife was transporting his body from Denmark, I was so worried. What if she can't? What will I do, if he can't return to Poland? So, I sat and cried… and prayed, waiting for him. Worried to death. But, then, my daughter came to me one night, and she was standing over me. I got frightened. I asked, 'What do you want?' But she said, 'Don't worry, Mama, everything will be fine. I'm watching over everything. You'll get your Rafał back'. And then she was gone, just vanished. The next day, they brought his body back.

In Randia's fictional worlds, her characters care for the dead spirits, just as the spirits care for them. The above scene, however, goes beyond Randia's imaginings of how spirits and humans might care for one another to the material practices of establishing that reciprocal care, such as feeding and providing assurance and company. Randia, like many Catholic Roma in Poland with whom I have worked, believed in an afterlife and that spirits inhabit our realities and guide our lives. She maintained that her deceased children's spirits watched over and cared for her. In fact, she said, it was only her children's spirits who ever truly cared. 'Nobody cares anymore', she said, continuing: 'when my family was here, I still was looked after, but now they don't care anymore. They have their own problems, and they are far. If I dropped dead, no one would notice. Well, I shouldn't say no one, because my son and daughter who died would. They care. They always pay attention'. Like Córka's visits from Bożena, Randia had experienced nightly visitations after her children died. She was pleased to be receiving these visitations because, as evident above, she believed that the spirits really cared and 'paid attention' to her life when no one else did. She told me how her late daughter, Mariola, came to fetch food for herself:

> My daughter comes at night, usually around 3 am. I'm sleeping... in deep sleep, and then she comes to the kitchen, rummages through cupboards, looking for food. She comes for food because she had died hungry. That's why she comes! She couldn't eat, poor thing. She was so sick she couldn't eat for weeks. At first, she was very loud. She'd scare the wits out of me! I'd jump out of bed and even scream. She was angry, I know. She hated how she died in pain and hunger. [...] But there wasn't always food in the kitchen. Sometimes I simply just wouldn't have any. Didn't go shopping or – like when I'm feeling ill, I don't go fortunetelling then and can't buy food. So, she'd be angry, poor thing. But then, when I knew she was coming for food, I'd cook up a meal and leave it there. She'd always take it. I know it's her, because who else would? There's no one here. And I sense her there... I know she's there. When I hear her steps in the kitchen, it's her. Cause that's how she'd always walk.

In another scene, Córka makes crepes with cottage cheese, sour cream, and sugar. Randia, as narrator, tells the audience that crepes were one of Córka's favorite dishes. She explains that Córka would make 'the best crepe dough ever, so good that it would make your mouth water!' The day of the scene, Córka was able to make many crepes because cottage cheese was on sale. I interjected and asked Randia for whom Córka was making the crepes, whether she was expecting any guests. Randia pondered and – slowly rubbing her chin – replied that there were no specific guests that would visit Córka that day. She 'just made crepes like she always had done when the cottage cheese was on sale'. When I asked what would happen to all this food if no one came, she replied that someone would always come and, if not, Córka would eat it herself or Bożena would come. 'And others [other children] would come too', insisted Randia. 'Why wouldn't they come? They miss their mother just as much as she misses them. They look out for her, if she needs them, if she wants anything... they keep guard'.

Many a time Randia stressed that she really enjoyed cooking for her family, and that she missed having her family around. She admitted that she would still, occasionally, prepare larger meals like she had always done. At least on two occasions I had witnessed Randia cooking an extensive dinner when not expecting any visitors. One afternoon, she showed me how well she had prepared cabbage rolls, doing so deftly despite her blindness. I remember that day vividly. She wore a white apron inside out over a black blouse with lace around the collar. There were pieces of cabbage scattered all over her apron and the blouse. 'I know I'm filthy', said Randia, 'but it doesn't matter. I have a washing machine. But look what I've made! I've already eaten several cabbage rolls with such relish!' When I asked Randia who would eat all those cabbage rolls, she said that she certainly would; but on another occasion, she confided in me:

> Cooking makes the time pass. What else am I supposed to do? Sometimes, I'll prepare food and wait. Perhaps someone will stop by? Then I can offer them a bite to eat. You know, a good meal is so important. My daughter died hungry, so she comes for food. Nearly every night I wake up and hear her in the kitchen rummaging through the cupboards, looking for food. So, I make food. And wait. If no one comes, my daughter will come. The one who died last year. She always does.

Randia's performances of the impossible demonstrate how performance ethnography can stage a place where 'the real, banal, messy, faltering ways in which …' transformative action can proceed 'with not too much fuss' (Horton and Kraftl 2009, 14). The slow-motion activism in my project did not rely on an explicit understanding of politics and change (Horton and Kraftl 2009, 14), but emerged as performative creativity somewhere from the depths of grief and magical thought. While it is challenging to trace the flow of power between the global and the intimate, I argue that performance ethnography can reveal how intimate, embodied imaginings of the future can be central players in – not merely passive victims of – geopolitical processes. Slow-motion activism can be an important intimacy politics (Pain and Staeheli 2014) that builds bonds of reciprocity, undoing customary divisions between global/local, private/public, real/fictional, and human/spirit worlds. Such a politics constitutes hopeful and powerful, embodied stances generated by 'the necessity to survive and improve a dignified life' (Bayat 2000, 547). Individuals and communities can intervene in their lifeworlds not only through grandiose political actions but also by mobilizing magical thought, creating impossible worlds where there is still another life in which one's child may survive.

Notes

1 At the same time he cautions that such a 'public discussion' can never be viewed outside of its politics of power, that is to say, how the performance 'enables, sustains, challenges, subverts, critiques and naturalises' ideology, and how the performance 'accommodate[s] and contest[s] domination' (Conquergood 1991, 190).

2 Bertolt Brecht (1898–1956) was a poet, theatre practitioner, theoretician, and playwright who developed 'epic theatre', which aimed at the politicization of audiences by inviting them to engage in social critique and action. Brecht's epic style of acting is characterized by, among other elements, actors stepping in and out of character, shifting roles, playing more than one character, and addressing the audience directly. All of these strategies aimed at staving off the audience's empathy and, instead, inviting them to rational thought.
3 In Russian theatre director and theoretician Konstantin Stanislavski's psychological realism, the actor 'steps into' and emotionally identifies with the character portrayed.
4 See, for example: https://www.huffpost.com/entry/what-losing-your-mother-feels-like_b_6495618

References

Appadurai, Arjun. 1996. *Modernity at Large: Cultural Dimensions of Globalization*. Minneapolis: University of Minneapolis Press.

Bakhtin, Mikhail. 1986. *Speech Genres and Other Late Essays*. Translated by Vern W. McGee. Austin: University of Texas Press.

Bayat, Asef. 2000. "From 'Dangerous Classes' to 'Quiet Rebels': Politics of the Urban Subaltern in the Global South." *International Sociology* 15 (3): 533–557.

Clarke, Kamari M. 2010. "Toward a Critically Engaged Ethnographic Practice." *Current Anthropology* 51 (Supplement 2): S301–S312. DOI: 10.1086/653673.

Cohen-Cruz, Jan. 1998. *Radical Street Performance: An International Anthology*. New York: Routledge.

Conquergood, Dwight. 1985. "Performing as a Moral Act: Ethical Dimensions of the Ethnography of Performance." *Literature in Performance* 4: 1–13.

_____. 1988. "Health Theatre in a Hmong Refugee Camp: Performance, Communication, and Culture." *The Drama Review: A Journal of Performance Studies* 32 (3): 174–208.

_____. 1998. "Beyond the Text: Toward a Performative Cultural Politics." In *The Future of Performance Studies: Visions and Revisions*, edited by Sheron J. Dailey, 25–36. Washington, DC: National Communication Association.

_____. 2002. "Performance Studies: Interventions and Radical Research." *The Drama Review – A Journal of Performance Studies* 46 (2): 145–156.

Crapanzano, Vincent. 2004. *Imaginative Horizons: An Essay in Literary-Philosophical Anthropology*. Chicago: The University of Chicago Press.

Culhane, Dara. 2011. "Stories and Plays: Ethnography, Performance and Ethical Engagements." *Anthropologica* 53 (2): 257–274.

Denzin, Norman K. 2003. *Performance Ethnography: Critical Pedagogy and the Politics of Culture*. Thousand Oaks, CA: Sage.

Didion, Joan. 2005. *The Year of Magical Thinking*. New York: Alfred A. Knopf.

Elliott, Danielle and Dara Culhane. 2016. *A Different Kind of Ethnography: Imaginative Practices and Creative Methodologies*. Toronto: University of Toronto Press.

Fabian, Johannes. 1990. *Power and Performance: Ethnographic Explorations through Proverbial Wisdom and Theater in Shaba, Zaire*. Madison: University of Wisconsin Press.

Geertz, Clifford. 1973. *The Interpretation of Cultures*. New York: Basic Books.

Gilchrist, Alison. 2000. "The Well-Connected Community: Networking to the 'Edge of Chaos'." *Community Development Journal* 35 (3): 264–275.

_____. 2009. *The Well-Connected Community: A Networking Approach to Community Development*. Bristol: Policy Press.

Hackney, Fiona, Hannah Maughan, and Sarah Desmarais. 2016. "The Power of Quiet: Remaking Affective Amateur and Professional Textiles Agencies." *Journal of Textile Design Research and Practice* 4 (1): 33–62. DOI: 10.1080/20511787.2016.1256139.

Hemment, Julie. 2007. "Public Anthropology and the Paradoxes of Participation: Participatory Action Research and Critical Ethnography in Provincial Russia." *Human Organization*, 66 (3): 301–314.

Horton, John and Peter Kraftl. 2009. "Small Acts, Kind Words and 'Not Too Much Fuss': Implicit Activisms." *Emotion, Space and Society* 2 (1): 14–23.

Irving, Andrew 2011. "Strange Distance: Towards an Anthropology of Interior Dialogue." *Medical Anthropology Quarterly* 25 (1): 22–44.

_____. 2018. "A Life Lived Otherwise: Contingency and Necessity in an Interconnected World." *Anthropologica* 60 (2): 390–402. DOI: 10.3138/anth.2017-0003.

Jasinka-Kania, A. (2009). Exclusion from the nation. *International Journal of Sociology*, 39(3), 15–37.

Johnston, Barbara Rose. 2010. "Social Responsibility and the Anthropological Citizen." *Current Anthropology* 51 (S2 Engaged Anthropology: Diversity and Dilemmas): S235–S247.

Kazubowski-Houston, M. (2011). Thwarting binarisms: Performing racism in postsocialist Poland. *Text and Performance Quarterly*, 31(2), 169–189.

Kazubowski-Houston, M. (2017). Quiet theater: The radical politics of silence. *Cultural Studies ⇔ Critical Methodologies*, 18(6), 410–422.

Kazubowski-Houston, Magdalena. 2010. *Staging Strife: Lessons from Performing Ethnography with Polish Roma Women*. Montreal and Kingston: McGill–Queen's University Press.

_____. 2012. "A Stroll in Heavy Boots: Studying Polish Roma Women's Experiences of Ageing." *Canadian Theatre Review* 15: 16–23. DOI: 10.1353/ctr.2012.0054.

_____. 2017. "Agency and Dramatic Storytelling: Roving through Pasts, Presents, and Futures." In *Anthropologies and Futures: Researching Emergent and Uncertain Worlds*, edited by Juan Francisco Salazar, Sarah Pink, Andrew Irving, and Johannes Sjöberg, 209–224. London & New York: Bloomsbury Academic.

_____. 2018. "An Elephant in the Room: Tracking an Awkward Anthropology." *Anthropologica* 60 (2): 413–426.

Kazubowski-Houston, Magdalena and Virginie Magnat. 2018. "Introduction: Ethnography, Performance, and Imagination." *Anthropologica* 60: 361–374.

Kline, Nolan and Rachel Newcomb. 2013. "The Forgotten Farmworkers of Apopka, Florida: Prospects for Collaborative Research and Activism to Assist African American Former Farmworkers." *Anthropology and Humanism*, 38 (2): 160–176. DOI: 10.1111/anhu.12016.

Maddrell, Avril. 2018. "Living with the Deceased: Absence, Presence and Absence-Presence." *Cultural Geographies* 20 (4): 501–522.

Madison, D. Soyini. 2005. *Critical ethnography: Method, Ethics, and Performance*. Thousand Oaks, CA: Sage.

_____. 2010. *Acts of Activism: Human Rights as Radical Performance*. New York: Cambridge University Press.

Massumi, Brian. 2002. *Parables for the Virtual: Movement, Affect, Sensation*. Durham, NC: Duke University Press.

Mittermaier, Amira. 2011. *Dreams that Matter: Egyptian Landscapes of the Imagination*. Berkeley: University of California Press.

Osterweil, Michal. 2013. "Rethinking Public Anthropology through Epistemic Politics and Theoretical Practice." *Cultural Anthropology* 28 (4): 598–620. DOI: 10.1111/cuan.12029.

Pain, Rachel and Lynn Staeheli. 2014. "Intimacy Geopolitics and Violence." *Area* 46 (4): 344–360.

Pottinger, Laura. 2017. "Planting the Seeds of Quiet Activism." *Area* 49 (2): 215–222.

Powiatowy Urząd Pracy w Elblągu: STOPA BEZROBOCIA 2010-2015. Accessed October 2015. Retrieved from http://www.elblag.up.gov.pl/kategorie/248

Rosaldo, Renato. 1989. *Culture & Truth: The Remaking of Social Analysis*. Boston: Beacon Press.

Salazar, Juan Franscisco, Sarah Pink, Andrew Irving, and Johannes Sjöberg, eds. 2017. *Anthropologies and Futures: Researching Emerging and Uncertain Worlds*. New York: Bloomsbury Publishing, Inc.

Schechner, Richard. 1985. *Between Theatre and Anthropology*. Philadelphia: University of Pennsylvania Press.

Sjöberg, Johannes. 2018. "An Epistemology of Play – Provocation, Pleasure, Participation and Performance in Ethnographic Fieldwork and Filmmaking." *Anthropologica* 60 (2): 403–412. DOI: 10.3138/anth.2018-0061.

Turner, Victor and Edith Turner. 1982. "Performing Ethnography." *The Drama Review: A Journal of Performance Studies* 26 (2): 33–50.

Sime, Jennifer. 2007. "'The Prickly Beards of Shepherds and the Peeled Moon and the Fly…': Locating and Dislocating Lorca's *Duende*." *Irish Journal of Anthropology* 10 (2): 44–49.

White, Anne. 2011. *Polish Families and Migration Since EU Accession*. Bristol: The Policy Press.

9

BIG DATA, THICK DATA, DIGITAL TRANSFORMATION, AND THE FOURTH INDUSTRIAL REVOLUTION: WHY QUALITATIVE INQUIRY IS MORE RELEVANT THAN EVER

Julianne Cheek

Introduction: What Is This Chapter About?

Put succinctly, this chapter is a conversation about why making connections between digitization, digitalization, a fourth industrial revolution, people-in-context, and qualitative inquiry matters. This is an important discussion to have in an era of rapid technological development that has seen the relentless digitization of people's daily life. Such digitization, digitalization, and the digital transformation that arises from them are constantly changing connections between people, places, and organizations. On a daily basis, all sectors of society—businesses, industry, governments, and education—are called on to digitally transform in order not to be left behind as we enter a fourth industrial revolution (Schwab 2016).

Yet, despite the growing prominence of terms such as digitization, digitalization, and digital transformation in such calls, there is a lack of consistency, and clarity, in how these terms are used and understood (Irniger 2020). For example, digitization and digitalization are used as synonyms, or it is assumed that digitalization *is* digital transformation. In part, this blurring has arisen from, and reflects, the rapid evolution and development of this field (Chapco-Wade 2018). Since the discussion that follows will use all of these terms at various times, it is important to briefly clarify how they are used. To do so, I offer my working definitions[1] of these terms for the purposes of this chapter, while recognizing the wider contestation, and often confusion, over how these terms are defined/ understood/used (Brennen & Kriess 2016). With this caveat in mind, when I use the term "digitization" I refer to the process of converting information from analog to a digital form. The information itself does not change, and nor does the purpose for which that information is used. What *does* change is the form in which that information is available—for example, "books turned into e-books, paper information turned into electronic formats and digital processes, music in bits and bytes, the list goes on" (i-Scoop Accessed 27/9/2020).

Such digitization enables digitalization. However, while digitalization relies on the digitization of information, it refers to much more than simply the form that specific pieces of information take (i.e., analog or digital). It is when digitization is used to turn interactions, communications, business functions, and models into digital versions of themselves that *digitalization* occurs (Carlsson 2018; Gartner 2020a, 2020b). Hence, digitalization is not simply a technical enterprise as digitization is. Rather, it is a socially situated and constructed process, made up of complex connections between the technology enabling both the digitization and the digitalization, the organizations and groups of people interacting with that technology, and the specific context in which the digitalization is occurring. It is about people-in-their-context, not just people-in-relation-to-technology. In other words, digitalization does not occur in isolation from the individuals and organizations that participate in it, or from the contexts in which that participation occurs.

Digitization and digitalization underpin the digital transformation that demarcates what Schwab (2016) called a fourth industrial revolution. Indeed, digitized data has been described as being "the propulsive energy behind this fourth industrial revolution—playing the same role as coal, oil and electricity did in the previous revolutions" (Mulkers 2017). We will take a closer look at the idea of a fourth industrial revolution and the digital transformation driving it in the next section.

The Third and Fourth Industrial Revolutions and the Rise of Data As a Commodity

The third industrial revolution was "catalyzed by the development of semiconductors, mainframe computing (1960s), personal computing (1970s and 80s) and the internet (1990s)" (Schwab 2016. p. 7) leading to "widespread change beginning in the 1980s with PCs and the internet" (Saldanha 2019, p. 6). In many cases, however, the result of this was that "processes were streamlined, not revolutionized: they were the same analog processes, duplicated in digital form" (Siebel 2019, p. 14). This provided more efficient and effective ways of working, but only within those existing models and the thinking underpinning those models.

In 2016 the founder and Executive Chairman of the World Economic Forum, Professor Klaus Schwab, introduced the idea of a fourth industrial revolution. This was a revolution that Schwab envisaged providing a new chapter in human development, driven by the increasing availability, convergence, and interaction of a set of technologies enabling digital transformation. Such digital transformation marks "[t]he migration of enterprises and societies from the Third to the Fourth Industrial Revolution era" (Saldanha 2019, p. 7). This fourth industrial revolution is demarcated by:

- The speed of its evolution, a major driver of which is "the availability of massive computing capacity at negligible and further plummeting costs… [such] increasingly pervasive and inexpensive digital technology is causing widespread industrial, economic and social change…[and] has occurred only in the past decade or two" (Saldanha 2019, pp. 6–7).
- Its breadth and depth. For example, the increasing "melding of the physical, digital and biological worlds today…[such that] what used to be physical (e.g., retail stores) can be digital (e.g., online shopping), or what used to be purely biological (e.g., traditional medicine) can be biotech (e.g., personalized genetic medication)" (Saldanha 2019, p. 6).
- The unprecedented size and scope of these changes. As Schwab notes, the fourth industrial revolution is not only a change in "what we do but also who we are. It will affect our identity and all the issues associated with it: our sense of privacy, our notions of ownership, our consumption patterns, the time we devote to work and leisure, and how we develop our careers, cultivate our skills, meet people, and nurture relationships… The list is endless because it is bound only by our imagination" (Schwab 2016, p. 97).
- Being as much about the social contexts to which we are connected, and within which we construct our daily reality, as it is about technology and digitized data. This is a revolution characterized by the intersections between people *and* digital transformations in context, and the recognition that "digital disruption is fundamentally about people" (Kane et al. 2019, p. 239).
- The potential to result in changes "so profound that, from the perspective of human history, there has never been a time of greater promise or potential peril" (Schwab 2016, p. 2).

Read collectively, and making the connections between them, these dot points highlight that the fourth industrial revolution is about much more than simply having access to more, bigger, faster, or the "latest" (for a few minutes anyway) technology. Rather, the disruption and transformation (i.e., the "revolution") emerges from the intersection(s) of rapidly developing technology *and* the way that people interface with that technology in their social contexts *and* what that interface enables or leads to in those contexts. In the next section I develop this point and look at the contribution that qualitative inquiry can make to better understanding these intersections.

Complex Connections: The Importance of Putting People, Their Contexts, and Qualitative Inquiry into the Digital Mix

Schwab (2016) observes that the digitization and digitalization that enables the fourth industrial revolution impact in unpredictable ways on "economy, business, governments and countries, society and individuals" (Schwab 2016, p. 28). This reinforces the point made above: namely, that digital transformation is not simply the development and use of the technology that enables it. Rather, it is a socially situated and constructed process that takes place in a social space (Cheek 2003) made up of complex connections between the technology, the participants, and the social context in which the transformation is occurring. This space is constantly (re)negotiated based on understandings of what, for example, digitalization is and is for—understandings that are brought to that space by the various stakeholders and participants interacting with and within it (Barker & Jane 2016).

People in that space who are the subjects of—and, at times, subject to— that digitalization choose what part they will/can play in that space. At various times, and sometimes at the same time, they may choose to be an active/passive/ resistant player with respect to different aspects of this digitalized space. For example, they may embrace some technologies while resisting others. At other times, others may choose for them what part they will, or even can, play— sometimes resulting in them being excluded from an aspect of this social space, with the result that the ability to optimize the perceived benefit of the digitalization is lost. A good example of this is provided by the COVIDsafe tracking app launched by the Australian government in April 2020.

The COVIDsafe tracking app "uses encrypted Bluetooth communications to note phones within 1.5 m of one another for at least 15 minutes. If a person with the app is later diagnosed with coronavirus, they can share that information with state health authorities so their close contacts can be warned" (Dudley-Nicholson 2020, p. 6). Individuals were encouraged to download the app and use it to help control the spread of the virus. However, installing the app required iOS 10 software on Apple iPhones and Android 6.0 and above. This assumed that everybody had the latest, or relatively recent, phones or devices. Unfortunately, research showed that "more than 900,000 Australians were still using smart phones running incompatible software by the end of 2019. This was confirmed by figures from StatCounter and Statista" (Dudley-Nicholson 2020, p. 6).

Thus, while having an app to facilitate tracking of close contacts of people who later tested positive for COVID-19 might have been a good idea, the developers needed to think a lot more about the social spaces into which the app would be rolled out. This included how people in those contexts would (or even could) interface with that technology. The COVIDsafe tracking app roll-out highlights the importance of shifting the focus in digitalization from the development of technological capability and instead putting it on people's interactions with that technology. This includes the ways in which digitalization happens and why (Cheek & Øby 2019), how it is thought about and why (Cheek 2017), is felt and why (Lupton 2017), and is made sense of and why (Madsbjerg 2017) *by people-in-context*. Yet these considerations are often relegated to the margins of an area that has historically been, and continues to be, dominated by a technical/technological focus.

The key point in all this is that while technology may enable digitalization, or even a digitally driven disruption and/or transformation, in itself it cannot determine how that digitalization and/or disruption happens—or even if it happens at all. As Kane and colleagues remind us, digital disruption (or "digital" anything, for that matter) is "fundamentally about people" (Kane et al. 2019 p. 239). How and/or whether it happens depends on the constantly negotiated and fluid positions taken up by various stakeholders in relation to that technology and its effects. For, as Markham sagely observes,

> digital never stands alone as a topic of inquiry. As a modifier for some other concept, digital operates metonymically to stand in for countless modes of interaction, types of information, platforms for interaction, and cultural formations…It is high time to move beyond 'digital' as the default modifier, grammatically and conceptually speaking, especially because to be useful at all, the term must be defined each time it is used, to identify the specificity of meaning within context.
>
> *(Markham 2018, p. 513)*

Therefore, what is truly interesting is the social spaces that emerge when these two ideas—digital and that to which it refers—meet *and are integrated in some way*. This is what the fourth industrial revolution is about, and it is this integration that will determine how the digital transformation integral to that revolution plays out.

When the fourth industrial revolution is viewed in this way, the potential contribution that qualitative inquiry can make to understanding this digital transformation in context is profound, central, and far-reaching. Qualitative inquiry can, and must, act as a correction to what is often an over-emphasis on the technical side of digitalization and a resultant lack of emphasis on the human interface with the consequences of that digitalization. Further, it is imperative that this happens now. The fourth industrial revolution is in its early days, "which provides human kind with the opportunity and responsibility to shape not just the design of new technologies but also more agile forms of governance and positive values that will fundamentally change how we live, work and relate to each other" (Schwab & Davis 2018, p. 17).

To act as this correction, and to contribute new and different ways of thinking about all things digital, qualitative inquiry must claim a central place *in its own right* in conversations and dialogue about the fourth industrial revolution and digital transformation. For, after all, qualitative inquiry has developed from many years of scholarship and research exploring and understanding people in context. Such scholarship and experience can be, and needs to be, applied to the macro and micro societal context(s) and social spaces arising from digital transformation.

By placing people at the center, rather than the margins, of these conversations, the dialogue is refocused on digital transformation in relation to humans in *their* context(s), and not just humans in relation to the context(s) defined for them by that digital transformation. As Christian Madsbjerg, founder and director of a strategy consulting company with high-profile companies and industries among its clients, notes,

> at the end of the day, it doesn't matter how much hard data we have in our hands, how many brain scans we have monitored on our screens, or how many different ways we have segmented our markets. If we don't have a perspective on the human behavior involved, our insights have no power.
>
> *(Madsbjerg 2017, p. x)*

In the next section I develop the point made by Madsbjerg that without a perspective on, and understanding about, the human behavior involved, our digitally produced data and the insights derived from them have no power. To do so I will use the idea of big data, a major driver, and enabler of digital transformation in the era of a fourth industrial revolution, as the vehicle for the discussion.

Big Data—the New "Must-have" (Even If You Are Not Sure What to Do with It or Why)

Big data has become a contemporary buzzword and a "must have" for governments, businesses, and individuals not wanting to be left behind—even though where "behind" and therefore "ahead" are is not always crystal clear. Indeed, Richards and King declare that we are "on the cusp of a 'Big Data Revolution,'" the scale of which "is such that all kinds of human activities and decisions are beginning to be influenced by big data predictions, including dating, shopping, medicine, education, voting, law enforcement, terrorism prevention, and cybersecurity" (2014, p. 393). This revolution is about awareness: "[t]he analysis of big data sets gives us greater awareness of the world that lets us make predictions and solve problems" (Richards & King 2014, p. 405).

Big data is made up of millions of digital traces (Latour 2007) that each of us generate in the course of our daily lives when we interact in some way with technology, or, as Latour puts it, "upload our former selves into these virtual worlds" (2007, p. 129). It is a direct consequence of digitization and is a "massive, rapidly changing and heterogeneous digital amalgam" (Thompson 2019, p. 208). For example, every time we log on to our computer, answer our smart phones, send a text, visit social networking sites, get captured on street cameras, or track our heart rate when exercising, we generate digital traces. Digital traces are also generated by our passports, credit cards, clothing, and pets if they have a certain type of microchip implanted in them (see Mills 2018). Also generating digital traces are "internet of things" (IoT) devices, defined as "nonstandard computing devices that connect wirelessly to a network and have the ability to transmit data" (WhatIs.com n.d.).

However, spelling out exactly what big data *is* is not easy. It has become one of those taken-for-granted, used-by-everyone phrases, that Richards and King (2014) term "catchall" phrases. Richards and King (2014) also point out that which definition of big data is in use, and what is emphasized in that definition, reflects who is doing the defining. For example, from a technological perspective big data is often defined narrowly, using technically oriented definitions such as that for a collection of data to be considered big data, is must be big in volume (terabytes, petabytes, or even exabytes[2]), big as in containing a wide variety of data types, and big as in the amount or volume of data produced/processed per unit of time (often known as the "3 Vs": volume, velocity, and variety). An example of this type of definition is: "Big data is high-volume, high-velocity and/or high-variety information assets that demand cost-effective, innovative forms of information processing that enable enhanced insight, decision making, and process automation" (Gartner 2018c).

A different view of big data is offered by boyd and Crawford, who understand Big Data as "a cultural, technological, and scholarly phenomenon…[that l]ike other socio-technical phenomena…triggers both utopian and dystopian rhetoric" (2012, p. 663). This understanding decenters technical, data-centric 3-V definitions and views of big data, and instead emphasizes the interplay of:

1. *Technology*: maximizing computation power and algorithmic accuracy to gather, analyze, link, and compare large data sets
2. *Analysis*: drawing on large data sets to identify patterns in order to make economic, social, technical, and legal claims
3. *Mythology*: the widespread belief that large data sets offer a higher form of intelligence and knowledge that can generate insights that were previously impossible, with the aura of truth, objectivity, and accuracy. (boyd & Crawford 2012, p. 663)

In this understanding of big data it is the interconnection and interplay between all of these dimensions (points 1 to 3) that makes a collection of digital traces big data, not just having a high volume of data in the form of digital traces (i.e., point 1 in isolation). In themselves the digital traces are not data; rather, they are a form of "digital exhaust—the data trails produced by online digital activities, related or not" (Peirce et al. 2019, p. 3). Elements of this digital exhaust might be able to be used as data, but that will depend on how, and why, they are used (i.e., points 2 and 3). This is why Clive Humby pointed out, when introducing the metaphor of data as the new oil, that "data is the new oil. It's valuable, but if unrefined it cannot really be used" (see Haupt 2016).

Building on this statement by Humby, it is important to remember that the data traces that make up any collection of big data are decontextualized. For example, from a digital trace we may know that someone made a mobile phone call but we do not know why, what was said and/or happened during that phone call and/or after it. Big data cannot tell us this. In fact, all it can tell us is the fact that the activity occurred—the digital trace. The social context in which the trace was produced is missing. This is because the data were not collected in context and, therefore, the interpretation of that data cannot take into account that context. The emphasis on, and priority given to the word "Big" can hide many inadequacies in the data. This is a point often overlooked in the rush for, and euphoria about, "Big Data."

Equally important to remember is that no data, including big data, can be understood apart from the researcher who has collected, assembled, and interpreted that data. It is the researcher who decides what will be collected and called data, as well as how it will be collected and analyzed. These subjective decisions are made by all researchers, including those who program the algorithms that drive the analysis of big data. Such decisions reflect particular views about the nature of the reality that is being researched (ontological considerations), what we can know about that reality, and how we can know it (epistemological considerations). This reminds us that data is not a fixed "thing" (Markham 2018) but, rather, is "fluid, a chameleon, able to take different 'shades' of meaning based on the perspective of the researcher" (Koro-Ljungberg 2016, p. 47).

Despite this, "at times, the pursuit of big data is driven by the epistemic assumption that expansive data sets offer superior forms of intelligence and erudition—a view that has been challenged in the existing literature" (Mills 2018, p. 592). All researchers (quantitative and qualitative), leaders and managers, practitioners of various sorts, and citizens basing their decisions on this data should be aware and wary of this drift toward new forms of "the bigger the amount of data the better the data" type of thinking. Thompson terms this the "latest incantation of the quantitative-methodology-as-magic-bullet myth" (2019, p. 209)—a refracted form of positivist and post-positivist thinking. This has led to new forms of "data-ism—the assumption that technology can always do better than humans" (Mills 2019, p. 3), based on the further assumption "that technically generated digitized *data*, is more objective or more reliable" than nontechnically generated data, and that somehow its "'bigness' renders obsolete the need for robust theory to interpret the data" (Mills 2019, p. 3). This series of assumptions ignores the fact that "the value of data is not tied to the data itself, but to what questions can be answered by that data" (Mills 2018, p. 596). This important point, and what happens when it is ignored, is the focus of the next section.

Made-up People? Big Data and Algorithms

Algorithms are integral to the analysis, and therefore to the use, of big data. In fact, Latzko-Toth, Bonneau and Millette (2017, p. 199) define big data as "the algorithmic processing of very large sets of 'traces' of user activities collected by digital platforms—so-called 'Big Data.'" Put simply, an algorithm is a methodical set of steps that can be used to make calculations, resolve problems, and reach decisions. The word

> [is] commonly used nowadays for the set of rules a machine (and especially a computer) follows to achieve a particular goal. It does not always apply to computer-mediated activity, however. The term may as accurately be used of the steps followed in making a pizza or solving a Rubik's Cube as for computer-powered data analysis.
>
> *(Merriam-Webster Dictionary n.d.)*

Thus, an algorithm is the fixed set of steps followed to make calculations and conclusions based on a very specific set of programmed parameters. The calculations are precise and rigorous *within the parameters of that algorithm.* Such bounded precision and rigor mean that the calculations, and the conclusions that are based on them, are not necessarily correct or useful outside those parameters. The algorithm is unable to take into account the social context or space in which the digital trace was produced—the *"What is it like to be this person? How do they experience their world?"* (Madsbjerg 2017, p. 104—emphasis in original) type of thinking needed to provide rich and thick interpretation.

The assumption that technology can always predict what humans will do, or how they will think about something, can cost individuals, organizations, and governments millions of dollars and create significant stress and injustice for people. The Australian government agency Centrelink found this out the hard way. What has become known as the "Robodebt" fiasco (see Henriques-Gomes 2020) is an excellent example of precise, rigorous, algorithm-based analysis leading to imprecise, non-rigorous, and just plain wrong decisions!

Centrelink is part of Services Australia,[3] the Australian government entity charged with providing a range of health, social, and welfare payments and services through a number of programs.[4] The Australian government, like many governments, as part of responsible fiscal management, attempts to stop welfare/ social support overpayment and/or fraud. From mid-2016, Centrelink employed algorithmic analysis to issue automated debt notices to recover what it claimed were overpayments, or incorrect payments, made to welfare recipients. Debt notices were issued where the algorithmic calculations concluded individuals had under-reported their fortnightly income levels when receiving a welfare benefit. The conclusion that these fortnightly income details were under-reported was based on crossmatching them with data from the Australian Taxation Office (ATO) about the individual's total yearly income.

In such crossmatching the yearly income reported to the ATO was used to calculate an average fortnightly income for the year. This could then be cross-referenced to the fortnightly amounts reported by the welfare recipients to Centrelink to reveal whether income was being under-reported (Stilgherrian 2017). Between 2015 and 2020, more than 300,000 people (Hayne 2020) received automated debt notices and letters of demand to repay the government, based on the result of an algorithmic calculation. This calculation had determined that the income declared in the tax returns of these people, when averaged across the 26 fortnights comprising the tax year, did not match the income they declared to Centrelink in the specific fortnights of that year when receiving their benefit. The conclusion was that the person had cheated the system by not declaring all of that fortnightly income, and therefore should not have received the level of welfare support that they did. Automated debt notices were sent to people whom the algorithm flagged, accompanied by demands for payment and threatening debt collector involvement and possible legal action.

However, what this algorithmic data analysis did not, and could not, take into account is that people are individuals and exist in social contexts that may change over time. The algorithm (like any algorithm) could not deal with, or make sense of, what Madsbjerg terms "the mess of real-world data" (2017, p. xv) because it had not been set up to do so. Dividing annual income into 26 equal fortnightly amounts did not reflect real-world situations in which individuals' circumstances changed during the year—for example, losing one's job after earning a high wage for the first part of the year, or studying for only part of the year and working for most of it. In effect, Centrelink had "lost touch with the humanity of their customers and their constituents and, as a result, they…[mistook] numerical representations and models for real life" (Madsbjerg 2017, p. xiv). As a result, the conclusions that were reached were often just plain wrong—even though the algorithm was right, at least in terms of correctly processing the data according to the parameters used to program it.

From the time that the data were crossmatched and analyzed, through to the time that the repayment demands were made, there was no direct human oversight of, or involvement in, the decisions being made on the basis of that algorithmic analysis. But there was a large human cost, as the comments and stories from those receiving letters of demand on the website #NotMyDebt attest. For example: "I have paid that despite the fact that I knew I did not owe it, I did not want the stress and anxiety—just working to make ends meet as it is" (#NotMyDebt n.d.). There were allegations that incorrect debt notices had led to mental health issues and even cases of suicide among recipients (Hayne 2020).

What was the end result? This chain of events resulted in the threat (and, as of the time of writing, the ongoing possibility) of a class action against the Australian government.

> The essence of the Robodebt Class Action is that debts raised by Centrelink's Robodebt System are unlawful, and all recipients should be compensated by the Respondent to the claim, the Commonwealth of Australia (which is responsible for Centrelink). The Robodebt Class Action argues that Centrelink's use of averaged ATO information to reassess a recipient's entitlements does not provide a valid basis to allege that the recipient has been overpaid and owes a debt.
>
> *(Gordon Legal n.d.)*

Further, in mid-2020 the Australian government announced that it expects "that most of the unlawfully raised debts paid under the [R]obodebt scheme will be refunded by November, with the $721 million to start heading back into the pockets of welfare recipients from July 1" (Whyte 2020).

The take-home message from this example is that algorithm-driven analysis, while it may be right, can lead to wrong conclusions being drawn. This emphasizes a key point—namely, that big data is not just "made," but is "made up," in the sense of putting millions of digital traces together in new and different ways that are, in turn, used to "make up" people—a form of the idea of making up people put forward by Hacking (1985). People and their circumstances are "made up" by certain configurations of big data (thereby becoming algorithmic selves) and then profiled in some way. In effect, people become a particular data double, and this double then becomes the "real them" until they can prove otherwise.

This is despite the fact that when making up people we can categorize people in wrong ways, we can miss trends, we can misinterpret what the analysis tells us, and, equally importantly, what it cannot tell us. Peirce et al. (2019, p. 79) liken this to Plato's allegory of the cave, "where what was viewed appeared real, but was a shadow of reality. Big Data provides a worldview that is a reflection of everyone but of no one." This is a point that has been made by many in the past, but given recent events such as the Robodebt fiasco—or the A-level exam results controversy in the UK[5]—it is obviously a point that still needs to be made.

In the light of such fiascos and controversies, attention has turned to how to make algorithmic analysis "thicker" by adding contextual considerations to it in some way. One suggestion for how this might be done is by the use of what is termed "thick data." In the next section I take a closer look at this suggestion and the questions it raises for qualitative inquiry.

Thick Data: A Possible Solution or Part of a "Mashing" Problem?

In 1985, Robert Stake observed that "case study data have been called 'thick data,' not necessarily stacked high, but 'thick like spaghetti,' highly interconnected" (Stake 1985, p. 279). His spaghetti metaphor captures the idea of data-in-context. This is a context made up of a tightly wound series of interconnections in which none of those connections, or the data related to them, can be understood in isolation (the equivalent of being served your spaghetti strand by strand).[6]

In an era of increasing interest in "Big Data," Wang (2013) has been prominent in promoting the use of thick data in corporate arenas to counter a growing loss of focus on context, and the person-in-that-context, in the corporate rush to collect and analyze more and more data and produce more and more algorithmic customer data doubles. In one of the earliest references to thick data in relation to Big Data, Wang (2013) wrote:

> Lacking the conceptual words to quickly position the value of ethnographic work in the context of Big Data, I have begun, over the last year, to employ the term Thick Data (with a nod to Clifford Geertz!) to advocate for integrative approaches to research.

Note that Wang points out that her understanding of thick data involves "a nod" to Clifford Geertz. She is aware that there much more to this term than a common-sense use or understanding. This is an important point, as Geertz never explicitly used "thick data" as a term. Rather, he emphasized the enterprise of "thick description," noting that it was not "techniques and received procedures that define the enterprise. What defines it is the kind of intellectual effort it is: an elaborate venture in, to borrow a notion from Gilbert Ryle, 'thick description'" (Geertz 1973, p. 6). Thus, influenced by Ryle's idea of "the description of intellectual work" (1971, p. 305), which Ryle termed "thick" description,[7] Geertz overtly locates the notion of thick description as being thick not in terms of its data, but in terms of the intellectual work that underpins it.

Hence, thick description is not a thing to be "got" as an end in itself. Rather, it is inextricably linked to the intellectual work of "thick interpretation" (Denzin 1989). For, as Denzin notes of "thick description," "(1) It gives the context of an act; (2) it states the intentions and meanings that organize the action; (3) it traces the evolution and development of the act; (4) it presents the action as a text that can then be interpreted (see Denzin 1989, p. 33). This idea is captured well by Ponterotto (2006, p. 543): "Thick description refers to the researcher's task of both describing and interpreting observed social action (or behavior) within its particular context."

On the other hand, a *"thin description* simply reports facts, independent of intentions or the circumstances that surround an action" (Denzin 1989, p. 33, emphasis in original). Thin description is, therefore, unable to move beyond a description of a fact—for example, that a digital trace exists. It cannot explain why that digital trace is there, or how it came to take the form that it does (think back to the Centrelink example discussed previously). Thin description is unable to take into account that "online experience is at all times tethered in some fashion to off-line experience" (Jones 1999, p. xii). Consequently, it is unable to perform the intellectual work of thick interpretation (Denzin 1989). For, as Schwandt (2001, p. 255) points out,

> to thickly describe social action is actually to begin to interpret it by recording the circumstances, meanings, intentions, strategies, motivations, and so on that characterize a particular episode. It is this interpretive characteristic of description rather than detail per se that makes it thick.

This is the case even if we have terabytes, petabytes, or even exabytes of data. Thick description, and the thick interpretation it enables, can complement and enhance conclusions reached from the algorithmic analysis of big data. However, what it cannot do is make a big collection of thin data—that is, the actual digital traces *themselves*—thicker, by thickening those actual traces in some way. Instead what thick description and interpretation *can* thicken, or provide more depth to, is the partial analysis and interpretation of a situation or context provided by algorithmic analysis of that big collection of thin data. This point builds on Markham's important observation that

> [o]ne type of response to the rise of data, datafication, and big data has been to defend ethnographic research within the discursive frame of data, insisting that ethnography is about "small data," "all ethnography is big data," or "big data just needs thick data"…these responses …yield epistemological ground, so that the whole baseline for appropriate ethnographic inquiry shifts to a new register.
>
> *(Markham 2017, p. 8)*

Similarly, Thompson (2019, p. 207) notes that the current infatuation in marketing and business schools with big data as "a technological holy grail" operates to discount theories and methodologies from areas such as anthropology, sociology, critical history, gender studies, and literary criticism. He observes that one suggested avenue to address such discounting is the idea of thick data:

> academic marketers have opportunistically argued that 'thick data' is the necessary complement to big data, and therefore has a pivotal role to play in business schools' data analytic-oriented missions…the ideological frame of the big data myth becomes the governing structure for these instrumental applications of cultural analyses".
>
> *(Thompson 2019, p. 217)*

An example of such opportunism in action being the assertion from Valero that the "anthropologists, sociologists and social scientists of tomorrow must learn to defend what they know how to do and the added value that their studies can bring to companies and organizations…Thick Data is a cover letter, a concept that we should commit to and popularize among all" (Valero 2017).

In all of this the key issue is whether the emergence, evolution, and consolidation of "thick data" as a term in the big data lexicon is an example of qualitative research yielding epistemological ground. Have thick description and thick interpretation been reduced to what Koro-Ljungberg (2016, p. 7) calls "easily digestible overviews," in the form of "thick data" that, in turn, has been reduced to the status of a cover letter? Does this consolidate thin ways of thinking about qualitative inquiry and reduce thinking about such inquiry to considerations of how it can be used to assist something else—in this case, "thickening" of thin big data?

Epistemologically thin ways of thinking are exemplified by a note that accompanies WordSpy's (2020) definition of thick data, which states: "This term is a mashup of *big data* and *thick description*, an anthropological research methodology that documents not only human behavior, but also the context of that behavior." Such a definition can certainly lead to qualitative research yielding epistemological ground, if terms such as thick description and thick interpretation are co-opted, mashed up, and then mashed in with other terms without considering what that overall "mash up" does to the ideas and understandings that underpin each of those terms.

This is particularly so when much of this "mashing" is being driven, and very rapidly, by adopters of technology in business and industry with an eye to gaining a commercial and market edge. Such adopters often may not know, or even consider it necessary or relevant to know, who or what a nod is being given to and why that matters. They want fast information and agile thinking exemplified by the fact that digitized blogs and discussion papers of ideas such as "thick data" routinely display the time needed to read them. For example, see the "three-minute reading time article" on thick data by Broscow (2020), one of many similar "articles" proliferating even as I write this chapter, and no doubt as you read it. All of which is exacerbated by the promotion and consolidation of a "bits and bytes" mentality in digitalized times.

Therefore, the big question that arises from this, and that requires our urgent attention, is how to proactively prevent our qualitative inquiry, and the ideas and understandings central to it, being reduced to easily digestible "morsels"—calling cards or cover letters, devoid of the thinking that gives qualitative inquiry its power. Could this lead to a situation in which qualitative inquiry is "subsumed within a larger paradigm of data science, whereby a qualitative perspective is seen to contribute merely a type of analysis...(or in the context of thick data even merely a type of data to be used to thicken or support other data)... rather than a world view" (Markham 2018, p. 520)? This would be a situation analogous to the "protracted eclipse" and "subaltern position" that Agamben saw politics undergoing, because "by losing sight of its own ontological status, it has failed to confront the transformations that gradually have emptied out its categories and concepts" (Agamben 2000, p. ix).

Agamben's description of emptied-out categories and concepts reminds us why it is important to push back against the colonization of qualitative inquiry by new forms of datafication, or the reification of data. Datafication as exemplified by statements such as "(t)hick data allows us to provide a dimensional context for more complex interpretations. We take into account feelings, choices, experiences and degree of satisfaction. Big data describes facts, thick data explains them" (Der 2017). Such datafication loses sight of the fact that it is not actually the "big" data that describes facts, nor the "thick" data that explains them. Rather, in the case of "big" data it is the algorithm-based analysis that describes certain possible facts in a given parameter-bounded situation. Similarly, it is thick description and thick interpretation that do the explaining—not "thick" data.

Beginning to Round Off, Not End, a Discussion To Be Continued...

Qualitative inquiry has a long history of focusing on, and producing excellent scholarship about, the intersections of ethical, political, and social justice considerations that shape and are in turn shaped by the societal contexts in which those intersections occur. As Denzin and Giardina noted a decade ago in this series:

> While constant breaks and ruptures define the field/s of qualitative research, there is a shifting center to the project: the avowed humanistic and social justice commitment to study the social world from the perspective of the interacting individual.
>
> *(2011, p. 13)*

This includes the societal contexts that make up the social world produced by digital transformation. These rapidly developing contexts, and the social spaces within those contexts, are shaped by the complicated connections between digitization, digitalization, a fourth industrial revolution, and of course people-in-context.

By remaining true to this "avowed humanistic and social justice commitment to study the social world from the perspective of the interacting individual" (Denzin & Giardina 2011, p. 13), qualitative inquirers can push back against the emerging idea of a digital human self derived from, and therefore reduced to, a collection of data derived fragments. A data double that in some contexts defines, even becomes, what a person *is*. By pushing back in this way, we can make sure that the flood (not just spot) light is kept on emerging issues of data ownership, protection, security, sharing, privacy, and justice related to the use of big data to power the algorithmic analysis that produces those data doubles.

There is a need for constant diligence about, and increasing scrutiny of, these rapidly evolving ethical and social justice issues, which have a habit of morphing into new and refracted forms. For, as Mills observes:

> What is right or wrong use of data in research varies across times, cultures and context … No data generation and analysis can be free from complex ethical concerns, but the technological changes to the production, sharing, and repurposing of data raise new issues and pitfalls for social scientists who wish to harness big data [or for our purposes digital forms of data] for their scholarly purposes.
>
> *(Mills 2019, p. 56)*

Therefore, we need to know (a lot) more about human interface(s) with emerging technology, *and* what the impact of that interface is. To achieve this, we must decenter what has become at times a human–in-relation-to-technology type of thinking and, instead, put humans at the center: a technology-in-relation-to-humans thinking.

This is why qualitative inquiry is more relevant than ever in an age where our culture has never before "been so seduced by the promises of artificial intelligence, machine learning, and cognitive computing" (Madsbjerg 2017, p. xxi). This is because despite this seduction, people are, as they always have been, the real key to digital transformation (Kane et al. 2019). To counter such seduction, we need to remind ourselves, and others, that in many social situations "human intelligence is still the most efficient intelligence for addressing contextual challenges. It is an efficiency based not on scalable knowledge but on a profound understanding of the particular" (Madsbjerg 2017, p. 205).

The Take-home Message

Canadian Prime Minister Justin Trudeau stated half a decade ago in his special address to the World Economic Forum:

> New technology is always dazzling, but we don't want technology simply because it is dazzling. We want it, create it and support it because it improves people's lives… Technology needs to serve the cause of human progress.
>
> *(cited in Parker 2016)*

Similarly, we do not want big data, thickened thin data, small data, thick data, digitization, digitalization, or digital transformations simply because they are dazzling or the latest must-have brand. Rather, we want them because they contribute to improving people's lives in the contexts in which those lives are lived. Therefore, it is our duty and our responsibility as a community of qualitative scholars to actively contribute to the development of societal contexts, and social spaces within those contexts, that can combine the power of algorithms with the wisdom and experience of people.

Remembering this fact opens up unlimited opportunities for qualitative inquiry to make a difference, and to get on the front foot in the conversation about digital transformation. We must insist that we are part of that conversation, and thereby part of discussions about this historical moment that is the fourth industrial revolution, and its impact. Further, this participation must be on qualitative inquiry's terms and not those of others. We must actively resist any emptying out (Agamben 2000) of qualitative inquiry's categories and concepts. This means we must stop conceding ground to others—something that is already happening, as Linder's (2020) comment on Broscow's article on thick data (with a designated 3-minute reading time) indicates:

> It is about combining the WHAT, WHEN, WHERE and HOW OFTEN, stemming from Big Data, with the WHY and HOW stemming from Thick Data. Both combined gives you the full Picture and you can make sure that you rely on the Facts and not on the Guess. That's why Analytics and Market Research should walk hand-in-hand and not in a competitive manner.
>
> *(Linder 2020, capitalization in original)*

Note that in this response it is "Market Research," not "Qualitative Inquiry," that should walk hand-in-hand with Analytics to acquire a full picture of the why and how stemming from thick data.

We cannot stand aside and allow such erosion and colonization of the body of knowledge related to our qualitative inquiry. Nor should we wait to be asked, or told, what our contribution to conversations in the era of the fourth industrial revolution might be. Instead, we must put ourselves—and the possibilities offered by our qualitative inquiry—forward, assertively and proactively. We must work out where and how to do this and reach the audiences we need to reach. This may require us to rethink and expand the mediums and arenas we use to communicate our qualitative inquiry (not just easily digestible forms of it) to those audiences. For, as Denzin (drawing on Mills 2000) reminds us, "scholars have an obligation to write their way into historical moments. The failure to do so makes us complicit with the histories that too often go on behind our backs" (Denzin 2009, p. 39).[8]

Notes

1 Each definition in itself could be a chapter in length. This is compounded by the fact that the meaning of the terms (mainly in terms of their scope and focus) has changed as the field has advanced (see Chapco-Wade 2018).
2 A petabyte is a measure of memory or data storage capacity equal to 2 to the 50th power of bytes. There are 1,024 terabytes (TB)—or 1 million gigabytes (GB)—in a petabyte and 1,024 PB make up one exabyte (International Electrotechnical Commission 2020).
3 The establishment of Services Australia (the former Department of Human Services) as an executive agency in the Social Services portfolio was announced on 26 May 2019 and came into effect on 1 February 2020. Services Australia continues to deliver Medicare, Centrelink, Child Support payments and other government payments and services (Services Australia 2020).
4 Programs identified on the government website are those targeted at seniors, job seekers, students and trainees, families, carers, parents, people with disability, Indigenous Australians, and people from culturally and linguistically diverse backgrounds (Services Australia 2020).
5 For an overview of this latest debacle see Coughlan (2020).
6 For a good overview and discussion of the emergence of the term "thick data" and ways it has been presented and thought about, see Latzko-Toth et al. (2017).
7 Ryle (1971) wrote of "thick" description rather than "thick description."
8 This chapter was written as a substitute for the paper on the above topic that I was scheduled to present at the 2020 International Congress of Qualitative Inquiry (ICQI). I never got to present that paper, as the Congress was cancelled because of the global disruption caused by the Covid-19 pandemic. Like the intended presentation, the chapter aims to open up discussion and reflexive thinking about the issues presented. My hope is for the chance to engage in constructive critique and dialogue about the points raised in this chapter with participants (real and/or virtual) at the 2021 ICQI. I will be submitting an abstract to the Congress organizers proposing just that.

References

Agamben, G 2000, *Means without end: notes on politics*, University of Minnesota Press, Minneapolis, MN.

Barker C & Jane EA 2016, *Cultural studies: theory and practice*, Sage, Los Angele, CA.

boyd d & Crawford K 2012, "Critical questions for big data: provocations for a cultural, technological, and scholarly phenomenon," *Information, Communication & Society*, vol. 15, no 5, pp. 662–679.

Brennen S & Kriess D 2016, "Digitalization," in KB Jensen, RT Craig, J Pooley, & EW Rothenbuhler (eds), *The International Encyclopedia of Communication Theory and Philosophy*, Wiley, Hoboken NJ.

Broscow D 2020, *Leveraging thick data to understand what consumers truly want*, viewed 9 October 2020, Retrieved from https://www.researchworld.com/leveraging-thick-data-to-understand-what-consumers-truly-want/

Carlsson C 2018, "Decision analytics—key to digitalisation," *Information Sciences*, vol. 460, pp. 424–438.

Chapco-Wade C 2018, "Digitization, digitalization, and digital transformation: what's the difference?," *Medium*, October 21, viewed 9 October 2020, Retrieved from https://medium.com/@colleenchapco/digitization-digitalization-and-digital-transformation-whats-the-difference-eff1d002fbdf

Cheek J 2003, "Negotiated social space: a relook at partnership in contemporary health care," *Primary Health Care Research and Development*, vol. 4, no. 2, pp. 119–127.

Cheek J 2017, "The marketization of research: implications for qualitative inquiry," in NK Denzin & YS Lincoln (eds), *SAGE handbook of qualitative research* (pp. 322–340), Sage, Thousand Oaks, CA.

Cheek J & Øby E 2019, "'Getting attention:' creating and presenting the visible, online, researcher self," *Qualitative Inquiry*, vol. 25, no. 6, pp. 571–582.

Coughlan S 2020, "Why did the A-level algorithm say no?," *BBC News*, August 14, viewed 4 October 2020, Retrieved from https://www.bbc.com/news/education-53787203

Denzin NK 1989, *Interpretive interactionism*, Sage, Newbury Park, CA.

Denzin NK 2009, *Qualitative inquiry under fire*, Left Coast Press, Walnut Creek, CA.

Denzin NK & Giardina MD 2011, *Qualitative inquiry and global crises*, Left Coast Press, Walnut Creek, CA.

Der J 2017, "What are thick data?," *Medium*, November 6, viewed 9 October 2020, Retrieved from https://medium.com/@jder00/what-are-thick-data-6ed5178d1dd

Dudley-Nicholson J 2020, "Thousands can't use safety app," *The Advertiser*, May 6, p. 6.

Gartner 2018a, *IT glossary: digitalization*, viewed 30 September 2020, Retrieved from https://www.gartner.com/it-glossary/?s=Digitalization

Gartner 2018b, *IT glossary: digitization*, viewed 30 September 2020, Retrieved from https://www.gartner.com/it-glossary/?s=digitization

Gartner 2018c, *IT glossary: big data*, viewed 30 September 2020, Retrieved from https://www.gartner.com/en/information-technology/glossary/big-data

Geertz C 1973, *The interpretation of cultures. Selected essays*, Basic Books, New York, NY.

Gordon Legal n.d., *Robodebt class action*, viewed 30 September 2020, Retrieved from https://gordonlegal.com.au/robodebt-class-action/

Hacking I 1985, "Making up people," in TL Heller, M Sosna, & DE Wellbery (eds), *Reconstructing individualism* (pp. 222–236), Stanford University Press, Stanford, CA.

Haupt M 2016, "Data is the new oil – a ludicrous proposition. Natural resources, the question of ownership and the reality of big data," *Medium*, May 2, viewed 30 September 2020, Retrieved from https://medium.com/project-2030/data-is-the-new-oil-a-ludicrous-proposition-1d91bba4f294#.vjyvcwnp0

Hayne J 2020, "Robodebt refunds top $220 million as Social Services boss rejects suicide claims," *ABC News* [online], July 31, viewed 9 October 2020, Retrieved from https://www.abc.net.au/news/2020-07-31/robodebt-refunds-top-220-million-centrelink/12512310

Henriques-Gomes L 2020, "Robodebt court documents show government was warned 76 times debts were not legally enforceable," *The Guardian*, September 19, viewed

4 October 2020, Retrieved from https://www.theguardian.com/australia-news/2020/sep/19/robodebt-court-documents-show-government-was-warned-76-times-debts-were-not-legally-enforceable

International Electrotechnical Commission 2020, *Prefixes for binary mutliples*, viewed 9 October 2020, Retrieved from https://www.iec.ch/si/binary.htm

Irniger A 2020, *Digitization, digitalization and digital transformation: what's the difference?*, viewed 5 October 2020, Retrieved from https://www.the-future-of-commerce.com/2020/05/18/difference-between-digitization-digitalization-and-digital-transformation/

i-SCOOP n.d., *Digital twins – rise of the digital twin in industrial IoT and Industry4.0*, viewed 9 October 2020.

Jones S 1999, "Studying the net: intricacies and issues," in S Jones (ed.), *Doing internet research:critical issues and methods for examining the net* (pp. 1–28), Sage, Thousand Oaks, CA.

Kane GC, Nguyen Phillips A, Copulsky JR, & Andrus GR 2019, *The technology fallacy: how people are the real key to digital transformation*, The MIT Press, Cambridge, MA.

Koro-Ljungberg M 2016, *Reconceptualizing qualitative research: methodologies without methodology*, Sage, Thousand Oaks, CA.

Latour B 2007, "Beware, your imagination leaves digital traces," *Times Higher Education Literary Supplement*, vol. 6, no. 4, pp. 129–131.

Latzko-Toth G, Bonneau C, & Millette M 2017, "Small data, thick data: thickening strategies for trace-based social media research," in A Quan-Haase & L Sloan (eds), *The SAGE handbook of social media research methods* (pp. 199–214), Sage, London.

Linder, Alexander 2020, Comment on D Broscow *Leveraging thick data to understand what consumers truly want*, posted 15 May 2020, viewed 30 September 2020, Retrieved from https://www.researchworld.com/leveraging-thick-data-to-understand-what-consumers-truly-want/

Lupton D 2017, "How does health feel? Towards research on the affective atmospheres of digital health," *Digital Health*, vol. 3, 2055207617701276.

Madsbjerg C 2017, *Sensemaking: the power of the humanities in the age of the algorithm*, Little, Brown, London.

Markham AN 2017, "Ethnography in the digital era: from fields to flow, descriptions to interventions," in NK Denzin & YS Lincoln (eds), *The SAGE handbook of qualitative research* (5th ed., pp. 650–668), Sage, Thousand Oaks, CA.

Markham AN 2018, "Troubling the concept of data in qualitative digital research," in U Flick (ed.), *The SAGE handbook of qualitative data collection* (pp. 511–523), Sage, London.

Merriam-Webster Dictionary n.d., *Algorithm*, viewed 29 September 2020, Retrieved from https://www.merriam-webster.com/dictionary/algorithm

Mills CW 2000 (1959), *The sociological imagination*, Oxford University Press, New York, NY.

Mills KA 2018, "What are the threats and potentials of big data for qualitative research?" *Qualitative Research*, vol. 18, no. 6, pp. 591–603.

Mills KA 2019, *Big data for qualitative research*, Routledge, London.

Mulkers Y 2017, "Data is the fuel for AI, so let's ensure we get the ethics right," *Medium*, December 10, viewed 29 September 2020, Retrieved from https://medium.com/future-of-work/data-is-the-fuel-for-ai-so-lets-ensure-we-get-the-ethics-right-b15337e18081

#NotMyDebt 2020, *NotMyDebt Shared Stories*, viewed 29 September 2020, Retrieved from https://www.notmydebt.com.au/stories/notmydebt-stories/just-trying-get-ahead

Parker C 2016, *Leadership lessons from Canada's Prime Minister Justin Trudeau*, viewed 20 September 2020, Retrieved from https://www.weforum.org/agenda/2016/01/leadership-lessons-from-canada-s-prime-minister-justin-trudeau/

Peirce AG, Elie S, George A, Gold M, O'Hara K, & Rose-Facey W 2020, "Knowledge development, technology and questions of nursing ethics," *Nursing Ethics*, vol. 27, no. 1, pp. 77–87.

Ponterotto JG 2006, "Brief note on the origins, evolution and meaning of the qualitative research concept 'thick description,'" *The Qualitative Report*, vol. 11, no. 3, pp. 538–549.

Richards NM & King J 2014, "Big data ethics," *Wake Forest Law Review*, vol. 49, pp. 393–432.

Ryle G 1971, *The concept of mind*, Hutchinson and Co., London.

Saldanha T 2019, *Why digital transformations fail*, Berrett-Koehler, Oakland, CA.

Schwab K 2016, *The fourth industrial revolution*, World Economic Forum, Geneva.

Schwab K & Davis N 2018, *Shaping the fourth industrial revolution*, Currency, New York, NY.

Schwandt TA 2001, *Dictionary of qualitative inquiry* (2nd ed.), Sage, Thousand Oaks, CA.

Services Australia 2020, *About us*, viewed 30 September 2020, Retrieved from https://www.servicesaustralia.gov.au/organisations/about-us/our-agency

Siebel TM 2019, *Digital transformation: survive and thrive in an era of mass extinction*, Rosetta Books, New York, NY.

Stake R 1985, "Case study," in J Nisbet, J Megarry, & S Nisbet (eds), *World yearbook of education 1985: research, policy, and practice* (pp. 277–285), Kogan Page, London.

Stilgherrian 2017, *When algorithms turn evil: the Centrelink debacle*, viewed 29 September 2020, Retrieved from https://authory.com/Stilgherrian/When-algorithms-turn-evil-the-Centrelink-debacle

Thompson CJ 2019, "The 'big data' myth and the pitfalls of 'thick data' opportunism: on the need for a different ontology of markets and consumption," *Journal of Marketing Management*, vol. 53, no. 3–4, pp. 207–230.

Valero PM 2017, *What is thick data?*, viewed 29 September 2020, Retrieved from https://blog.antropologia2-0.com/en/what-is-thick-data/

Wang Y 2013, "Why big data needs thick data," *Medium*, May 13, viewed 29 September 2020, Retrieved from https://medium.com/ethnography-matters/why-big-data-needs-thick-data-b4b3e75e3d7

WhatIs.com n.d., *IoT agenda*, viewed 30 September 2020, Retrieved from https://whatis.techtarget.com/site/IoTAgenda

Whyte S 2020, "Robodebt refunds won't affect current Centrelink payments," *The Canberra Times*, 1 June, viewed 4 October 2020, Retrieved from https://www.canberratimes.com.au/story/6776684/robodebt-refunds-wont-affect-current-centrelink-payments/

WordSpy 2020, *Thick data*, viewed 3 October 2020, Retrieved from https://wordspy.com/index.php?word=thick-data

CODA

Sublime Resistance: Imagining Peace, Freedom, Health, Happiness, Community*

John M. Johnson

> If you don't know where you are going, any road will get you there.
>
> Lewis Carroll

For 16 years the International Congress of Qualitative Inquiry (ICQI) has met in May to interrogate, define, debate, and perform the cutting edges of our futures. Following Lewis Carroll's admonishment, we have imagined our futures. We have imagined the roads to get us there.

First, we imagine a peaceful world. We don't want nuclear annihilation or destruction by other kinds of bacterial, chemical, biological, or other dumb weapons. We don't want our cultures to be destroyed by insane wars which have killed over 100 million of our sisters and brothers in the 20th century alone. We want to work with our allies in a positive, constructive, collaborative, cooperative manner to accomplish these goals.

Second, we imagine safety in our communities. We do not want to be shot or killed, as in the more than 400 mass killings in 2019, as documented by the organization which tracks these. We do not wish to be victimized by violent or sexual crimes, but we also do not want our young men to be locked away in prisons for so long they learned to be socialized, or "prisonized," into criminal careers.

Third, we imagine effective health care, at prices comparable to those paid in all other developed countries. We want comprehensive programs for women's reproductive health, effective treatment systems for mental health, reversal of the trends of lowering our life spans, reductions of deaths from alcohol, drugs, and medical (maltreatment) interventions (which consistently claim more deaths than alcohol and drugs combined).

Fourth, we imagine reasonable protections from health pandemics or disasters. We want clean water, and effective measures to make our environments and climates sustainable. We want to reduce our carbon footprint, and further develop clean fuels and sustainable systems.

Fifth, we imagine secure borders and comprehensive immigration reform, which includes legal immigration to assist and develop the growth of our economy. We want immigrants, migrants, and refugees to be treated humanely and with respect. We want to continue our long cultural traditions of welcoming migrants, immigrants, and refugees.

Sixth, we imagine living free of unreasonable searches, seizures, or restrictions of our constitutionally guaranteed liberties and freedoms; of speech, movement, assembly, body, loving, politics, and so on.

The above statements are not my own, I plagiarized them, not from the progressive platforms of Democratic candidates for elected office, but from American polling data. Over 70% of all Americans favorably agree with all of the above points. We may have partisan conflict on strategies and tactics, but on these visionary goals, we have significant agreement among large percentages of American citizens. These beliefs, attitudes, and opinions of our fellow citizens are the foundational hopes of our progressive politics of societal and global transformation.

For about four decades American politics have been defined by "the Washington Consensus," the neoliberal belief that unfettered and "self-regulating" markets would allow "all boats to float higher," that faster economic growth would produce faster economic gains for all strata of society, that the fruits of growth would not only "trickle down" to the poorest, but to other nations as well. Despite its name, neoliberalism was not a brand or offshoot of liberalism, and this obvious truth produced a spate of books analyzing the "end of liberalism" as we knew it (by the likes of James Taub, Mark Lilla, Adam Gopnik, Jill Lepore, Joseph Stiglitz, Robert Kuttner, Roger Cohen, and many others).

The 2008 financial crisis and the climate crisis did not produce significant doubts about the truth or scientific foundation of neoliberalism, despite the widespread protests or demonstrations against its effects; anti-WTO, Occupy, Black Lives Matter, Women's Marches, #MeToo, anti-GMO, Dakota Access Pipeline, Keystone XL Pipeline, Sagebush, Citizens Climate Lobby, and many more. There were thousands of other protests at the state and local levels, commonly animated by a local situation or tragedy which brought citizens to the streets and digital platforms. These demonstrations, protests, or other forms of resistance are often *reactive* in nature, meaning that they arise only after a provocative situation, accident, or tragedy. A *proactive* vision is needed, says Naomi Klein (2017), whereby resistance is based on transcendent values which have stood the test of time. Only such a proactive vision will sustain the worlds we imagine for our children and grandchildren.

Peace and Personal Security

Hundreds of millions of our fellow humans have perished in war, over 100 million in "The Great War" (World War I and World War II) alone. It is self-evident that peace is a transcendent value, even if the major world religions do not affirm this, and are often complicit in war. One of the great ironies in our lives (of many) is that the so-called "losers" of The Great War (Germany, Japan) are today thriving democracies with strong anti-war cultures, while the so-called "winners" (Russia, China, U.S.) are further advancing to authoritarian and anti-democratic cultures, where "saber rattling" and "war mongering" are ingrained in the cultures, where the militarization of the culture is enhanced by a virulent politics of fear (Altheide, 2016, 2017). Actual military operations are common. Since the end of the World War II, the U.S. has bombed over two dozen countries without prior legislative authorization required by the Constitution. The Physicians for Social Responsibility estimate that we have killed about 1 million people in Iraq, plus another 220,000 in Afghanistan, and 80,000 in Pakistan. In the last year of Obama's presidency, he dropped 26,171 bombs, and more recently the U.S. has used over 2,800 drone attacks without any declaration of war (Bacevich, 2013, 2020). This new "push button warfare" has been augmented with "targeted political assassinations" (of Qassem Soliemani, among others). The U.S. has over 4,855 military bases, including 587 in 42 countries spread throughout the world; why?

Approximately 53 cents of every dollar in the 3 trillion dollar annual U.S. budget goes for some kind of military expenditure, and yet this obscene militarization of the budget is largely "off the table" in recent political debates, as Democrats and Republicans seek to carve and devour this sacred cow to their advantage, feeling confident that all Americans "support the military." The U.S. military budget is larger than the military budgets of the next eight developed countries. Cornel West (2017:xv) links this militarization to the larger moral crisis in the culture:

> The undeniable collapse of integrity, honesty, and decency in our public and private life has fueled even more racial hatred and contempt. The rule of Big Money and its attendant culture of cupidity and mendacity have so poisoned our hearts, minds, and souls that a dominant self-righteous neoliberal soulcraft of smartness, dollars, and bombs thrives with little opposition. The escalating military overreach abroad, the corruption of political and financial elites at home, and the market-driven culture of mass distractions on the Internet, TV, radio push toward an inescapable imperial meltdown, in which chauvinistic nationalism, plutocratic policies, and spectatorial cynicism run amok. Our last and only hope is

prophetic fightback – a moral and spiritual awakening that puts a premium on courageous truth-telling and exemplary actions by individuals and communities.

For years I have participated with the members of our local Veterans for Peace chapter, where we stage anti-war demonstrations and protests. We even created anti-war floats to participate in the annual Veteran's Day Parade each November, until the City of Phoenix ceded control of the parade to a private organization, which threatened police arrests and eventually expulsion. Our veteran anti-war stalwarts are few in number, and so we have recognized it is imperative for all those who work against war and violence, sexism, racism, bigotry, misogyny, homophobia, and all forms of bigotry, to reach out and join with others, to create allies, alliances, collaborations, and eventually larger social movements, as happened with the civil rights movement, the women's movement. The national Veterans for Peace organization will focus on the relations between militarization and the degradation of the climate at its 2020 convention in Albuquerque, NM, and our local VFP now has allies in the environmental and climate movements.

School shootings commonly garner media attention, but mass shootings (of three or more) are more common, and other forms of criminal violence endemic in many U.S. communities. Even though there were more than 400 mass shootings last year, as documented by the organization Gun Violence Archive which tracks such data, most of these do not gain national mass media coverage, but are reported in the local communities where they occur. More than 32,000 people died by gun violence last year (about 11,000 gun suicides, about 12,000 criminal killings, plus about 9,000 accidental gun deaths), a greater total than deaths for the major diseases (Johnson, 2016). If we allow our attention to remain at the national level, we "know" that all attempts at national legislation have failed, and the common story line attributes this to the political influence of the National Rifle Association (NRA). But this is very misleading, because at the state and local levels, there have been effective efforts to enact "common sense gun control" rules and laws, in over 30 states and 80 local communities. Even recent polling of NRA members show that 72% favor "common sense gun laws and regulations" (usually defined as background checks, prohibition of mega-magazines and "bump stocks," mental health screening of gun buyers, ending the gun show exemptions, restrictions of hollow-shell cartridges, red flag warnings, and so on). This is an excellent example of how the attitudes and feelings of U.S. citizens transcend the usual partisan categories, and serve to give hope to movement activists to work across partisan boundaries. If we build alliances and coalitions at the local level, bridging substantive issues or problems, then it is easier and more effective to mobilize a larger resistance or movement when local tragedies occur. We need "rapid response teams" for our local tragedies and disasters to quickly establish contacts with like constituencies from other areas and communities. If "all politics is local," we need to take that page from House Speaker Tip O'Neil's playbook for our own more effective resistance responses.

Health and Wellness

Our 2020 election campaign has been filled with the gloomy metrics of our broken health system, and many creative proposals to move toward effective solutions. In recent years more than 400,000 Americans have lost health coverage, and today rich Americans live 20 years longer than poor Americans. American men now have a life expectancy of men in Sudan or Cambodia. We would save over 21,000 children's lives if we just had the same mortality rates as the rest of the developed world. The costs we pay for health care and medications greatly surpass the countries of Western Europe. The more comprehensive proposals are not likely to be soon institutionalized, significantly because of the massive vested interests involved in the current system, but there is little doubt that a very strong majority of Americans desire an affordable and effective health-care system; polls consistently show the bipartisan nature of the citizen wishes. Again, it is important to reach out to other groups to build alliances and coalitions.

I am convinced about the importance of this because of my own activist and organizational failures. During my life I have founded or cofounded nine nonprofit organizations dealing with social justice issues, and as I look back upon my life I realize that two of those were altered and then folded into state government programs ("co-opted"?), six no longer exist in any form, and only one exists in recognizable form; Middle Ground Prison Reform, now operating 37 years, and Arizona's largest and most effective prison reform organization. I know that this "organizational atrophy" or "burn out" is common in other communities, but this does little to mitigate my sense of failure (to expand and share the leadership base, to build better communication networks, to think more seriously about how to build the sustainable financial foundations for longer-term success, and so on). In my community we have a group known as *Local to Global Justice,* which exists to bring social justice groups together. At their 19th annual conference at Arizona State University in February, 2020, common themes articulated the inter-relations of all forms of bigotry, racism, sexism, homophobia, violence/war, misogyny; very similar to our ICQI. One distinctive aspect of ICQI is that it brings together master story-tellers, who can and do contribute to social justice movements by telling new and different stories about injustice; for example, how nearly 32,000 Americans were shot to death in 2017, that Americans are 25 times more likely to be killed by a gun than people in other developed countries, that this gun violence costs more than $700 per American every year, and most of these costs are borne by our taxpayers and health systems. Since we know from our polling data that 93% of all Americans and 93% of all gun owners favor background checks and other commonsense gun controls, we need to tell this story in a manner which is inclusive of all perspectives.

A large bipartisan majority feels that health-care issues are most important in the 2020 election, and while there are some undaunted optimists who feel that a national health system is an historical inevitability (see, Harari, 2014; Pinker, 2018), because of the vast vested interests in the health-care industries, this conflict is bound to be a long haul in the U.S., probably extending over many future elections. This Congress can play a central role as a "hub," as the center of the hub-and-spoke-model advanced many years ago by Saul Alinsky (1971), to communicate our collective successes and failures as we return to our local communities, and join with our brothers and sisters to make an impact on local issues.

Climate Change and Environment

> This is what you should do; love the earth and the sun and the
> animals….give alms to everyone who asks, stand up for
> the stupid and the crazy, devote your income and labor
> to others….argue not concerning God….
>
> Walt Whitman (1855)

> As crude a weapon as the cave man's club, the
> chemical barrage has been hurled against the fabric
> of life—a fabric on the one hand delicate and
> destructible, on the other hand miraculously tough
> and resilient, and capable of striking back in unexpected ways.
>
> Rachel Carson (1962)

Rachel Carson sounded a clarion call in her 1962 book *Silent Spring*, and today all of the developed nations have signed the Paris Accords, accepting our responsibility for the natural world. This will be an on-going and difficult process, extending for millennia. There are enormous vested interests involved in the exploitation of the environment; which others (Klein, 2019; Maddow, 2019; Wallace-Wells, 2019) have ably documented. Scientific evidence has now established an overwhelming impact of a dominant anthropogenic changes in our climate over recent decades (Weart, 2008), and most experts think the earlier predictions underestimated the potential impact (Wigley, 2020). Few if any at ICQI are climate scientists, but many of us have a crucial role to play. We are story-tellers, and we can tell and perform unique stories, because we know only too well that our history includes hundreds of years of oppressive myths and lies, hypocrisy, moral and political corruption. Our race-based caste system was and is based on the arrogant and myopic exploitation of our environment.

My Johnson ancestors arrived at Jamestown in 1616, a total of 23 family members led by John Johnson, who had a contract with the James Trading Company, to work and till the land for seven years, near Jockey's Neck and Corrowaugh Swamp across the James River from Jamestown. This led to an initial grant of about 200 acres, which family members extended and farmed for over 200 years, until a small group migrated to Indiana in 1832–1833. My ancestors owned and used slaves in their farming enterprises, although they were early converts to the Quaker sect, and were among the first to relinquish their claims to slaves, long before the 1861–1865 Civil War. In the oral telling of my family myths, there is often pride in this Quaker commitment, freeing of the slaves, and later in participating in the Underground Railroad (1830–1865) in Indiana. Only much later in my life did I learn about the genocide and settler colonialism which had decimated the many indigenous tribes around the Chesapeake Bay, near the Jamestown colony (Dunbar-Ortiz, 2014; Kelly, 2018), and then continued with the westward move into The Ohio Territory, which included Indiana, Kentucky, Illinois, parts of Michigan. So the lesson is clear; our lives and family histories are never-ending projects, the stories are never complete, but in need of continuous revision. In my case, the gifts and privileges I inherited were tied to our larger national stories about the violent destructions of the native peoples, the violent appropriation of their lands, and the awful history of chattel slavery. So what many outsiders would perhaps see as my "lily white," privileged ancestry is deeply stained with slavery and the blood of many others; the economic and material development of the U.S. is similarly stained, which means that our current environmental, ecological, conservation, and climate problems are intimately tied in with our very personal and family stories. This should be no news to those who attend ICQI, because such intimate contradictions provide the materials for some of our hallowed stories, such as Bud Goodall's (2006) stunning late-life discovery that his parents Harold Lloyd Goodall and Naomi May Alexander Saylor Goodall were clandestine CIA agents for their entire career, or Carolyn Ellis' (2009) classic *Revision*, where she revises and updates several of her earlier published stories, and argues that our stories are never complete, but exist only to be later altered or revised. This is how we at ICQI can contribute, to tell better and better stories, ones which integrate our personal narratives into the larger societal, cultural, historical, global contexts.

The diversity of our Congress produces the strength and value of our stories. We bring together interpretivists, postmodernists, poststructuralists, feminist, critical, post-Black, racial-ethnic, hybrid, queer, differently abled, indigenous, nonbinary, and everyone else on any margin; a global community which is intellectual, operational, and ethical (see, Denzin, 2010). We see the liminality of our experience in the world, and thus know that our stories and performances will never by exhausted by the categories used by social science. This is the spirit we communicate in our pedagogy, to invite our students to push against all racial, class, and gender boundaries to achieve the gift of freedom.

Love and Community

> Love is the vital essence that pervades and permeates, from the center to the circumference, the graduating circles of all thought and action. Love is the talisman of human weal and woe; the open sesame to every soul.
>
> Elizabeth Cady Stanton (1860)

Love is the most important part of our lives. Our love lives are complicated, and linguistically we discern our love of ancestors, parents, siblings, half-siblings, uncles, aunts, cousins, nephews, nieces, spouses, partners, friends, pets, colleagues, organizations (and their members), nations, physical objects, natural objects or phenomena, teachers, mentors, students, neighbors, and so on. Children deserve a special recognition, because from the first moment they serve as foundational teachers for the remainder of our lives. Our earliest love feelings center on family relations (if fortunate), and then begin to build from that foundation to expand to greater and more sophisticated love relations. Love does not eliminate sadness or suffering in life; indeed, some say these are inescapable ingredients. It is an uncertain but usually rewarding adventure. There is no fixed quantity of love for our life; the more we genuinely love, the more we become capable of genuine and true love. It is critical to recognize the role and importance of love in our lives, in order to better appreciate that all of these matters concerning politics and social policies are decidedly secondary in importance. Love is foundational; politics ephemeral. Love develops over the life span, helping us achieve a balanced and more simple accommodation to this difficult and challenging life; the lessons never-ending.

Our varied and complicated love lives teach us an important lesson, contrary to what our individualistic and materialistic culture often teaches, namely, we do not achieve happiness and meaning all by ourselves, commonly these are manifest in personal relations with others, which may include music, art, and sports cultures, where we interact with others in common purpose. We build our communities with these actions; community is what we *do* in these contexts of meaning. The idea that career success leads to personal happiness is one of the major "lies" promulgated by our culture, according to PBS and *New York Times* mainstay David Brooks. The reality is that meaning is communicated and experienced in relationships and communities. We are only as alone as we choose to be; we can be as involved as we want to be.

"Community" is a process, a verb, an ongoing project, dependent on our daily actions. Americans recognize the imperative to enforce borders and legal immigration and refugee processes, but the vast majority imagine America as a welcoming culture; many of our myths celebrate the "waves of immigration" responsible for helping build an industrial, then a technological, modern society. (These often involved racism, patriarchal misogyny, homophobia, and bigotry, true, but that is for storytellers at other ICQI sessions.) Each geographical area has a distinctive pattern; who would guess that Phoenix, Arizona, has large Somali and Nepali-Bhutanese communities?! It is important to think local-to-global, and build bridges across the categories of identity politics (often effectively using Federal or state laws), to create a larger unity of vision and purpose. George Lakey (2018: 165) writes:

> No system of domination can survive by coercion alone; it also uses division of labor. It socializes people into hierarchal groups that "specialize" in particular ways. The gender system in its Western cultural variation traditionally taught females to elevate their emotional and nurturing side while men lift up the ability to think rationally, fight, and provide. We see conflict around us now as that tradition is challenged. The age old stability of the patriarchy is now breaking down with consequent opportunity for people to break out of stereotyped roles.

The 2016 and 2020 national elections provide illustrative examples of competing theories of mass movements, and why they succeed or fail. In his 1971 book *Rules for Radicals* Saul Alinsky (1971) emphasized the crucial importance of organizing based on one-to-one personal relationships between the organizer and the people being organized, whereas in the 1977 classic *Poor People's Movements: Why the Succeed, How They Fail* Frances Fox Piven and Richard Cloward (1977) emphasize mass mobilization, and argued against efforts to institutionalize formal organizations (McNall, 2018:242-43). They additionally aver that the efforts to create formal social justice organizations often sap the emotional tonus of the demonstrations or protests, and often lead to either the co-option of the efforts, or the disappearance of the groups. The Bernie Sanders Presidential campaign clearly tried to combine both of these approaches, and Sanders often emphasized that his campaign was not a traditional elector campaign, but a social movement. Win or lose, this will be an illustrative example of how a movement succeeds, fails, is co-opted, or transformed. Electoral politics and social movements are rarely coterminous, and the longer view must extend far beyond the horizons of future elections.

Education and The Re-enchantment of the World

> Success in life is to be measured not so much by the position that one has reached in life as much as by the obstacles which he has overcome.
>
> *Booker T. Washington*

> Education is the most powerful force you can use to change the world.
>
> *Nelson Mandela*

Most of us at who attend ICQI would readily agree with the Nelson Mandela quote, and affirm that our lives have been fundamentally shaped by our formal and life education. Even if we were not classics or literature majors, we probably absorbed the classic view of education, namely, that our formal education provided a foundation of learning what our ancestors and predecessors thought and said, and this was an important but only a beginning of a lifelong process of learning, where our existential experiences in the world would be combined with and adumbrated by our continued reading, thinking, and experiences in our own culture, and progressive travel to and involvement with other cultures, culminating in an increasingly mature, but always incomplete and ongoing development. This may be where many of us began, but decades of neoliberal erosion have rendered this foundation near death; getting an education has been sliced and diced into the pragmatics of getting a job. *The Chronicle of Higher Education* recently published a series of essays on this demise, under the title "Endgame," (no longer a "crisis"), where distinguished authors discern the autopsy of this collapse. All of those attending ICQI over the last 16 years have lived this. We have presented many papers on this for 16 years. When I began my university teaching career, about 80% of college and university faculty were tenure or tenure-track; today it hovers around 33%. More than one million teachers now serve as nonpermanent staff, making up about 50% at public PhD-granting institutions, 55% of masters degree-granting institutions, 62% of the teaching staff at bachelors degree-granting places, 83% at community colleges, and 93% at for-profit institutions.

The growth of nonpermanent teaching staff tracks with the decline in public support for higher education, which dropped 26% between 1990 and 2010 (see, Mettler, 2018), and the stagnation of salaries, for most faculty, staff, and graduate students (Childress, 2018). My purpose here is not to revisit the devastation of neoliberal policies in higher education, but to suggest that we are now in a situation where most individuals in an institutional order which was at one time highly stratified are now similarly disadvantaged by the corporatization of the contemporary university system. The time is right for tearing down the status hierarchies and walls of the neoliberal university, and joining together with our university workers to build a more just institution for all parties involved (Newfield, 2019). Those of us with experience in social justice causes and campaigns can lead the way to building this more durable and more sustainable education community.

Creating or joining a new social justice group is exhilarating, energizing, consuming, joyous, significantly because the small founding group or core leadership group share a larger vision and purpose. The work and time commitment is intense, but everyone is energized by the larger shared purpose. Over time this commonly produces "burn out," and core members begin drifting away. In his book *Doing Democracy* (2001) Bill Moyer wrote about the different roles in social movement organizations, and encouraged individuals to become involved in ways consistent with their interests and personal desires, and later in *How We Win: A Guide to Nonviolent Direct Action* (2018) George Lakey revised Moyer's recommendations to four major roles: advocate, organizer, direct service, rebel. I would greatly expand this list; Leadership roles (Demonstration Leader, Strategist/Tactician, Board Chair/Member), Organization roles (Grant writer, Researcher, Consultant, Supporter/Fund Raiser, Event planners, Legal Consultants); Communication roles (Contact person, Blogger, Webpage custodian, Videographer, Twitterbug, Provocateur/Bird-dogger (disrupt politicians' speeches), Social Media, Observer); Support roles (Champion/Donor, Comedy Team performer, Dance Team performer, Trainer/Instructor, Security/Bodyguard, Marshall/Peacekeeper). For me, the roles I have played have varied by the organization, and throughout my life. When I began in my first protests as a student in the civil rights era, I was a foot-soldier and a follower. During my military service in Vietnam I continued to financially contribute to the organizations I had joined during my student years; I was a "paper member." In mid-life, I was more of an organizer, grant writer, and leader. And later I was pleased to play varied roles which would have been unlikely in my younger years; I recently participated with Contra-Tiempo, an Urban Latin Dance Theatre, a bold, multilingual Los Angeles-based dance company creating politically intense performances that imagine radical futures. In a different setting, in conjunction with the Bernard Osher Life Long Learning Program (OLLI) I helped write and then perform a social justice script for a local audience. We have diverse motives, emotions, and interests in joining with others, and these may change over time, as lives and circumstances change. The point is this; make your own personal assessment of your desires and emotions, then jump in and see what happens, always knowing a course adjustment or revision is possible at a later time.

Sociologist Kathleen Blee (2012) studied over 60 grass roots groups in Pennsylvania, including LGBTQ rights, Iraq war, the environment, guns, drugs, violence, school reform, animal rights, and many others. She focused on the dynamics of group formation, and found group boundaries continually change over time, sometimes the core founding group dissolves, and the group dies. But often the group members migrate to other related groups, and continue their struggle under a different banner, all the time debating and discussing goals, purposes, and visions. Protest groups often advance a symbolic imagination of alternate possibilities within a community, but this is rarely the same energy needed to populate, organize, and sustain a viable social movement organization over a longer term. Many of the older protest or activist groups provide many of the same social functions as a family, supporting and fostering a sense of meaning and belonging; a "safe haven" in an uncertain world.

To Resist Is to Exist

> Qualitative research scholars have an obligation to change the world, to engage in ethical work that makes a positive difference. They are challenged to confront the facts of injustice, to make the injustices of history visible, and hence open to change and transformation.
>
> *Norman K. Denzin (2010:115)*

This quote from Norman Denzin points to critical ties and linkages between our earliest religious forms and the secular forms of contemporary human rights and justice movements. The forms we think of as "religion" emerged in the range of 6,000 years ago, and these are commonly taken to be the sources of "transcendent meaning" in human life (Harari, 2014, 2016, 2018). Our ongoing and evolving histories show these forms to be intertwined with racism, sexism, inequality, oppression, war, violence, genocide, bigotry, discrimination, totalitarianism, torture, environmental degradation, abuse of animals, misogyny, executions, and arrogant moral absolutism in very complicated ways, producing great suffering. Each person today has some of these elements buried deep in their heart and soul, and it is imperative for each individual to discover and dissect these influences, in order to make a genuine and authentic commitment to love. As Cornel West said in a recent CNN interview, "Every American has some white supremacy buried deep within his or her heart or soul, including all Black Americans." We may be rooted in these histories, but not ultimately defined by or restricted by them (hooks, 2000). We can choose a different path. For me personally, I've had to resolve my own Quaker-Bretheran family history with the larger patterns of American history, to reconcile these with the racial, class, and gender structures of my upbringing and early adulthood, and accommodate all this within the decades of my Buddhist practice and study.

As we continue on this lifelong path of discovering our heart, we must come to grips with these regretful religious influences, to resist them nonviolently, with humility, to affirm the transcendent values identified earlier in this paper; peace, personal and family security, health, wellness, protecting and conserving the environment and climate, community, freedom, respect for others, inclusion, nonviolence, justice, happiness, and love. During the last decade this Congress has commonly drawn participants from 70 countries, drawn together not only by our common professional commitments to qualitative research and writing, but also by our desire to live in a diverse, intersectional, and queer world, where our personal behavior embodies a radical equality of respect for each individual. This is how we will re-enchant the world. This is the vision and imagination of sublime resistance.

CODA: A New World of Uncertainty

This paper was initially completed two days before the COVID-19 Coronavirus Pandemic changed the world. We don't know what will happen in the coming years. I hope for changes that are more peaceful and less violent, more green and less carbon, more inclusive, moving from aggression to compassion, greater personal and family security, more just and loving. But at this moment I am less hopeful than before.

Note

*This is dedicated to my late-life mentors: Daisaku Ikeda, Thich Nhat Hanh, and The Dalai Lama.

References

Alinsky, Saul, 1971. *Rules for radicals*. New York: Vintage.

Altheide, David L., 2016. *The media syndrome*. New York: Routledge.

Altheide, David L., 2017. *Terrorism and the politics of fear*, Second Edition. New York: Rowman and Littlefield.

Bacevich, Andrew J., 2013. *Breach of trust: How Americans failed their soldiers and their country*. New York: Holt.

Bacevich, Andrew J., 2020. *The Age of illusions: How America squandered its cold war victory*. Notre Dame, IN: Notre Dame University Press.

Blee, Kathleen, 2012. *Democracy in the making*. New York: Oxford University Press.

Childress, Herb, 2018. *The adjunct underclass: How America's colleges betrayed their faculty, their students, and their mission*. Chicago: University of Chicago Press.

Denzin, Norman K., 2010. *The Qualitative manifesto: A call to arms*. Walnut Creek: Left Coast Press.

Dunbar-Ortiz, Roxanne, 2014. *An indigenous peoples' history of the United States*. Boston: Beacon.

Ellis, Carolyn, 2009. *Revision: Autoethnographic reflections on life and work*. Walnut Creek, CA: Left Coast Press.

Goodall, Harold Lloyd, Jr., 2006. *A need to know: The clandestine history of a CIA family*. Walnut Creek, CA: Left Coast Press.

Harari, Yuval Noah, 2014. *Sapiens: A brief history of humankind*. London: Harvill Secker.

Harari, Yuval Noah, 2016. *Homo deus: A brief history of humans*. London: Harvill Secker.

Harari, Yuval Noah, 2018. *21 lessons for the 21st century*. London: Jonathan Cape.

hooks, bell, 2000. *Feminism is for everybody: Passionate politics*. Boston: South End Press.

Johnson, John M., 2016. "Guns as a symbol of (fill-in-the-blank)," *Cultural Studies—Critical Methodologies*, Vol. 16, No. 2, pp. 1–4.

Kelly, Joseph, 2018. *Marooned: Jamestown, shipwreck, and a new history of America's origin*. New York: Bloomsbury.

Klein, Naomi, 2017. *No is not enough*. Chicago: Haymarket.

Klein, Naomi, 2019. *On the burning case for a green new deal*. New York: Simon Schuster.

Lakey, George, 2018. *How we win: A guide to nonviolent direct action campaigning*. Brooklyn: Melville House Publishing.

Maddow, Rachel, 2019. *Blowout: Corrupted democracy, rogue State Russia, and the richest, most destructive industry on earth*. New York: Crown Publishing Group.

McNall, Scott G., 2018. *Cultures of defiance and resistance*. New York: Routledge.

Mettler, Suzanne, 2018. *Degrees of inequality: How the politics of higher education sabotaged the American dream*. New York: Basic Books.

Moyer, Bill, 2001. *Doing democracy*. Gabriola Island, B.C.: New Society Publishers.

Newfield, Christopher, 2019. *The great mistake: How we wrecked public universities and how we can fix them*. Baltimore: Johns Hopkins University Press.

Pinker, Steven, 2018. *Enlightenment now: The case for reason, science, humanism, and progress*. New York: Penguin.

Piven, Frances Fox, and Richard Cloward, 1977. *Poor people's movements: Why they succeed, how they fail*. New York: Random House.

Wallace-Wells, David, 2019. *The uninhabitable earth: Life after warming*. New York: Duggan.

Weart, Spencer, 2008. *The discovery of global warming*. Cambridge: Harvard University Press.

West, Cornell, 1993/2017. *Race matters*. Boston: Beacon Press.

Wigley, Tom M.L., 2020, "How good are past predictions of global warming," *Skeptical Inquirer*, Vol. 44, No. 2, March/April, pp. 45–49.

EDITOR BIOGRAPHIES

Norman K. Denzin is Distinguished Emeritus Professor of Communications, College of Communications Scholar, and Research Professor of Communications, Sociology, and Humanities at the University of Illinois at Urbana-Champaign, USA. One of the world's foremost authorities on qualitative research and cultural criticism, he is the author or editor of more than 30 books, including *The Qualitative Manifesto* (Routledge, 2009); *Qualitative Inquiry Under Fire* (Routledge, 2009); *Reading Race* (Routledge, 2009); *Interpretive Ethnography* (Routledge, 2009); *The Cinematic Society* (Routledge, 2009); *The Alcoholic Self* (Routledge, 2009); and a trilogy on the American West. He is past editor of *The Sociological Quarterly* (Routledge, 2009), co-editor (with Yvonna S. Lincoln) of five editions of the landmark *Handbook of Qualitative Research* (Routledge, 2009), co-editor (with Michael D. Giardina) of 17 books on qualitative inquiry, co-editor (with Lincoln and Giardina) of the methods journal *Qualitative Inquiry* (Routledge, 2009), founding editor of *Cultural Studies⇔ Critical Methodologies* and *International Review of Qualitative Research* (Routledge, 2009), editor of four book series, and founding director of the International Congress of Qualitative Inquiry.

Michael D. Giardina is Professor of Physical Culture and Qualitative Inquiry in the Department of Sport Management at Florida State University, USA. He is the author or editor of more than 20 books, including *Sport, Spectacle, and NASCAR Nation: Consumption and the Cultural Politics of Neoliberalism* (with Joshua Newman; Palgrave Macmillan, 2011) and *Qualitative Inquiry and the Politics of Resistance* (with Norman K. Denzin; Routledge, 2020). He is the co-editor of *Qualitative Inquiry* (Routledge, 2009), co-editor of *Cultural Studies ⇔ Critical Methodologies* (Routledge, 2009), co-editor of *International Review of Qualitative Research* (Routledge, 2009), co-editor of three book series on qualitative inquiry for Routledge, and Director of the International Congress of Qualitative Inquiry (ICQI). He is also the co-editor (with Norman K. Denzin, Yvonna S. Lincoln, and Gaile S. Cannella) of the *SAGE Handbook of Qualitative Research, 6th Edition* (Sage, forthcoming).

CONTRIBUTOR BIOGRAPHIES

Julianne Cheek is Professor in the Faculty of Business, Languages, and Social Sciences at Østfold University College, Norway. She is the author of *Postmodern and Poststructural Approaches to Nursing Research* (Sage, 2000). Her work has been published in *Qualitative Inquiry* (Sage journal); *Qualitative Health Research* (Sage journal); *Journal of Child and Family Studies* (Springer journal); *The Oxford Handbook of Multimethod and Mixed Methods Research Inquiry* (Oxford, 2015); and the *SAGE Handbook of Qualitative Research, 5th Edition* (SAGE, 2017).

Maria Dabboussy is a mother, a PhD Candidate in Geography, and a full time Administrator at Carleton University, Canada. Maria is also a Lebanese Canadian lover of all things food, theory, and critical thinking with kindness. As a student and someone who supports students, Maria is keenly interested in the practice of joy making in academic spaces. In research and life, Maria strives to incorporate intersectionality, critical race, and feminist practices.

Marcelo Diversi is Professor in the Department of Human Development at Washington State University-Vancouver, USA. He is the author of *Betweener Autoethnographies: A Path Toward Social Justice* (Routledge, 2018; with Claudio Moreira) and *Betweener Talk: Decolonizing Knowledge Production, Pedagogy, and Praxis* (Left Coast Press, 2009; with Claudio Moreira), which received the 2010 Book of the Year Award from the National Communication Association, Division of Ethnography.

Katie Fitzpatrick is Associate Professor and Head of School of Curriculum and Instruction in the Faculty of Education and Social Work at the University of Auckland, New Zealand. She is author of *Critical Pedagogy, Physical Education, and Urban Schooling* (Peter Lang, 2012), which received the 2013 Outstanding Book Award from the North American Society for the Sociology of Sport. She is also the editor of *Health Education: Critical Perspectives* (Routledge, 2014; with Richard Tinning), and co-editor of the Routledge book series "*Critical Studies in Health and Education*" (with Deanna Leahy, Jan Wright, and Michael Gard).

Katarina Georgaras is a PhD candidate in Geography at Carleton University, Canada, and a recent graduate of the Pauline Jewett Institute of Women's and Gender Studies MA program. Her research focuses on academic emotional geographies and geographies of dis/ability. She is passionate about accessibility, inclusion, and mental health.

Henry A. Giroux holds the McMaster University Chair for Scholarship in the Public Interest and is Professor of English and Cultural Studies. In 2002, he was named as one of the top fifty educational thinkers of the modern period in *Fifty Modern Thinkers on Education: From Piaget to the Present* as part of Routledge's *Key Guides Publication Series.* In 2019, he was named the winner of the Professional Freedom and Responsibility Award, given annually by the Association for Education in Journalism and Mass Communication (AEJMC) to writers who exemplify the principles of free expression, inclusivity, and media accountability. He is a regular contributor to a number of online journals including *Truthout, Truthdig, Boston Review,* and *CounterPunch.* He has published in many journals including *Social Text, Third Text, Cultural Studies, Harvard Educational Review, Theory, Culture, & Society,* and *Monthly Review.* He is on the Board of Directors for Truthout. His most recent books include: *Dangerous Thinking in the Age of the New Authoritarianism* (Routledge, 2016); *America at War with Itself* (City Lights, 2017); *The Public in Peril: Trump and the Menace of Authoritarianism* (Routledge 2018), *American Nightmare: Facing the Challenge of Fascism* (City Lights Books, 2018), and *The Terror of the Unforeseen* (Los Angeles Review of Books, 2019).

John M. Johnson is Emeritus Professor of Justice and Social Inquiry, School of Social Transformation, College of Liberal Arts and Sciences, at Arizona State University, USA. He has published eleven books and over 100 articles and chapters on topics such as existential and interactional theory, official corruption, domestic violence, religious crusades, qualitative methods, research ethics, justice theory, the death penalty, formal organizations, bureaucratic propaganda, drug laws, white collar crime, and prison reform. He has also been a visiting professor at the University of Paris and the University of Amsterdam.

Magdalena Kazubowski-Houston is an Associate Professor of Performance Studies at York University, Canada, where she is a co-founder of the Centre for Imaginative Ethnography (CIE), a project committed to advancing critical and politically conscious research. She is the author of *Staging Strife: Lessons from Performing Ethnography with Polish Roma Women* (McGill-Queens University Press, 2010), which received the 2011 Qualitative Book Award from the International Congress of Qualitative Inquiry. She trained as a theatre director with prominent Polish theatre/visual artist Józef Szajna and has worked as a professional theatre director, performer, and playwright in Canada and Poland.

Aaron M. Kuntz is Professor of Research Methodology and Department Chair of Counseling, Recreation, and School Psychology, at Florida International University, USA where he currently holds the Frost Professorship of Education and Human Development. He is the author of *Qualitative Inquiry, Cartography and the Promise of Material Change* (Routledge, 2018) and *The Responsible Methodologist: Inquiry, Truth-Telling, and Social Justice* (Routledge, 2015), which was selected as Honorable Mention for the 2017 AERA Qualitative SIG book award. Dr. Kuntz's latest book, *Qualitative Inquiry, Cartography, & the Promise of Material Change* (Routledge, 2019) was awarded the 2020 Outstanding Book Award from the Qualitative SIG at AERA.

Patrick Lewis is Professor of Early Childhood Education and Associate Dean, Faculty Development and Human Resources, at the University of Regina, Canada. His work as a storyteller-teacher-researcher has been published in such venues as *International Review of Qualitative Research; Journal of Childhood Studies; International Journal of Play; Journal of Social Science Education;* and the *SAGE Encyclopedia of Research Methods.*

Claudio Moreira is Professor of Performance Studies in the Department of Communication at the University of Massachusetts-Amherst, USA. He is the author (with Marcelo Diversi) of the award-winning *Between Talk: Decolonizing Knowledge Production, Pedagogy, and Praxis* (Left Coast Press, 2009) and *Between Autoethnographies: A Path toward Social Justice* (Routledge, 2018). His work has been published in *Text and Performance Quarterly; Qualitative Inquiry; Cultural Studies⇔Critical Methodologies;* and *International Review for Qualitative Research.*

César A. Cisneros Puebla is Professor at the University of Tarapacá, Arica, Chile. He has also been a visiting professor at the International Institute for Qualitative Methodology, University of Alberta, Canada, and in the CAQDAS Networking Project at University of Surrey, UK, as well as numerous Universities in South America. He received the 2020 Special Career Award in Qualitative Inquiry, which recognizes dedication and contributions to qualitative research, teaching, and practice from the International Congress of Qualitative Inquiry.

Sophie Tamas is Associate Professor of Geography and Environmental Studies, Emotional Geographies Lab, at Carleton University, Canada. She is the author of *Life After Leaving: The Remains of Spousal Abuse* (Left Coast Press, 2016). Her work has also been published in such venues as *Emotion, Space, and Society; International Review for Qualitative Research; Qualitative Inquiry; Feminist Studies;* and the *Handbook of Autoethnography.*

Jonathan Wyatt is Professor of Qualitative Inquiry and Director of the Centre for Creative-Relational Inquiry, at the University of Edinburgh, Scotland. Previously, he was Head of Professional Development at the University of Oxford, UK. He is the author of *Therapy, Stand-Up, and the Gesture of Writing: Towards Creative-Relational Inquiry*, which received the 2020 Qualitative Book Award from the International Congress of Qualitative Inquiry.

INDEX